DISCOVERIES

IN NON-FICTION

DISCOVERIES
IN NON-FICTION

Patricia Drapeau ✦ Jon Terpening ✦ Alex White

Discovery consists of seeing what everybody has seen
and thinking what nobody has thought.
Albert Szent-Gyorgyi Von Nagyrapolt

Toronto
OXFORD UNIVERSITY PRESS

Oxford University Press, 70 Wynford Drive, Don Mills, Ontario M3C 1J9
http://www.oupcan.com

Oxford New York Athens Auckland Bangkok Bogota Bombay
Buenos Aires Calcutta Cape Town Dar es Salaam Delhi Florence
Hong Kong Istanbul Karachi Kuala Lumpur Madras Madrid
Melbourne Mexico City Nairobi Paris Singapore Taipei Tokyo
Toronto Warsaw

and associated companies in
Berlin Ibadan

This book is printed on permanent (acid-free) paper ⊗.

Canadian Cataloguing in Publication Data

Main entry under title:
Discoveries in non-fiction

ISBN 0–19–540944–2

1. Readers (Secondary).   I. Drapeau, Patricia.
II. Terpening, Jon.   III. White, Alex, 1945–

PE1121.D58 1993   808'.0427   C93–093283–8

Some articles in this collection use the term "man" or "mankind" in the traditional
generic sense to include both men and women. The publishers recognize that the
terms "human" or "humankind" are preferable. The language of the original
articles, however, must be retained in the reprint.

Cover photo: Outline/PUBLIPHOTO
Cover background: First Light
Project Editor: Monica Schwalbe
Designer: Marie Bartholomew
Photo Researcher: Natalie Pavlenko Lomaga
Composition: Colborne, Cox & Burns/Ibex Graphic Communications

Printed and bound in Canada

3 4 5 6 — 01 00 99 98

CONTENTS

———◆———

MORE TO DISCOVER 159

ACKNOWLEDGEMENTS

Special thanks to the following educators who reviewed the manuscript at various stages:

Dai Ann Baynes, Burnaby North Secondary School, Burnaby, British Columbia

Barry M. Buckler, Lester B. Pearson Collegiate Institute, Scarborough, Ontario

Elizabeth Mitchell, Winston Churchill Collegiate Institute, Scarborough, Ontario

Carol Mayne-Ogilvie, St. Francis Xavier School, Edmonton, Alberta

Stefan Sierakowski, Lester B. Pearson Collegiate Institute, Scarborough, Ontario

Special thanks also to the following students who reviewed selections and provided us with their responses:

From Burnaby North Secondary School, Burnaby, British Columbia

Zaheer Abdulla	Sharon Chow	Anne Kan
Deepa Amin	Karen Chui	Richard Kim
Mark Banath	Chris Chung	Danny Ko
Ryan Barichello	Paul Chung	Paul Kojder
Christopher Bensler	Josh Cornell	Peter Kojder
Todd Burnie	Jason Crescenzo	Rachel Kong
Chris Car	Allison Davis	Loretta Lau
Johnny Chan	Alim Dhanji	Olivia Lau
Joseph Chan	Tavis Dunn	Denise Leon
Umar Chaudhry	Jonathan Fantillo	Sharon Li
Tracy Chen	Tanya Ferguson	Weddy Li
Calvin Cheng	Autumn Glowacki	Jonathan Lim
Peter Cheng	Farah Harji	Abbie Lu
Karen Cheung	Kristy Hayden	Tina Lutz
Mike Chisholm	Trevor Hunnisett	Jason Macaulay
Kylie Chow	Scott Johnson	Jimi Matilda

Acknowledgements

Thomas Mladenka	Raymond Power	Claudia Valiante
Michael Moniz	Ashlene Prasad	Saleena Vellani
Nery Monzon	Baljit Rathore	Aleem Virani
Giovanna Nardone	Ryo Sakai	Ante Vunic
Dawna Neufeld	Joe Scigliano	Tony Waring
Sabrina Nicoletti	Silvio Anthony Simon	Brent Watson
Irene Novinc	Christopher Stimson	Daniel Woodward
Ann O'Connor	Jennifer Syme	Felicia Yee
Julia Margaret Ogawa	Wendy Tarling	Dale Dalton Yoon
Vince Pau	Jamie Taylor	Geoff Young
Sylvia Pong	Lisa Truong	Tania Yuen

From St. Francis Xavier School, Edmonton, Alberta

Vanessa Aranas	Andrea Hamill	Lillian Ruta
Ryan Bebeau	Nancy Huynh	Angela Seguin
Peter Cigner	Rebecca John	Ben Steman
Claudio Dalle Ore	Joanne Marghella	Tara Strudwick
Katherine Della-mora	Ashley McClelland	Karen Tokarczyk
Kimberly Dolynchuk	Erin Merrick	Anna Vukovic
Tracy Ebach	Wijayanthi Navaratnam	Mark Wilson
Krystal Eliuk	Benila Ninan	Patrick Winski
Celine Gannon	Jay Pariti	Elaine Yakiwchuk
Carmen Grant	Monique Petrin	Saly Zachariah
Tracy Grant	Caria Renschler	

The students in the 1992–93 Grades 9 and 10 classes of Stefan Sierakowski at Lester B. Pearson Collegiate Institute, Scarborough, Ontario.

WHAT'S TO DISCOVER?

What is non-fiction? You probably think of newspaper and magazine articles based on factual reports and maybe essays. In fact, non-fiction writing can take many different and interesting forms. This book provides you with a sampling, a collection you can delve into following your own interests.

Where to start? Choose themes or articles that interest you. Then you can begin with some pre-reading activities. Pre-reading is something like stretching before working out, or knowing the terrain of a downhill ski run and anticipating the key parts before skiing. It's a way to gather your thoughts and ideas before you jump in, to make yourself feel more comfortable and be aware of what's to come. Here are some strategies you can use:

• Brainstorm all you know about a topic (e.g., spiders) before reading about it.
• Create a mind map for a topic. Then cluster some of the ideas from your mind map and write an opinion statement on the topic.

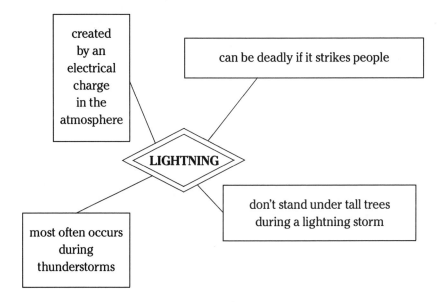

- Do some fast non-stop writing about a topic. What do you know, believe, or feel about the topic?
- Predict from the title of the selection what you think it will be about.
- Anticipate/predict some information that might be presented in the selection by jotting down three or four questions about the topic.

Don't worry. There are no right or wrong answers. This is just a way to get you thinking.

After you've read the selections, focus on your responses. Try keeping a response journal. As soon as you've finished reading a selection, jot down your initial responses as quickly as possible, preferably in sentence form. Write down reactions, questions, what you liked, learned or relearned, didn't like or understand, suggestions or questions to the author, or what you'd like to learn more about in relation to the topic.

After each selection in the book, you will also find a few open-ended questions. These are to provoke further thinking. Perhaps there's even more to discover!

SELF-REFLECTIONS

**We may as well go to the moon,
but that's not very far.
The greatest distance we have to cover
still lies within us.**
Charles de Gaulle

Have you ever watched athletes or explorers push themselves to the very limits of their endurance? Have you wondered why some people have devoted years to researching the lives of their ancestors or have written stirring accounts of how they have overcome difficult problems or periods in their lives? These people are involved in one of life's most mysterious and exciting pursuits—the search to determine who they are. This is one voyage of discovery each of us makes. The next time you stand in front of a mirror, take a close look at your reflection and think about how well you really know yourself. No explorer has ever travelled a more exciting journey that the one that goes on within us from the moment we are born.

TO CAST A SINGLE SHADOW:
THE ART OF GOING ALONE

Jeff Rennicke

"I had never been sprawled on my back six miles up a side canyon off the Colorado River with a severely twisted ankle before . . ."

With your eyes at ground level the stones in a dry desert creekbed shimmer with heat waves just like distant mountain ranges. It was something I had never noticed before, but then I had never been sprawled on my back six miles [almost 10 km] up a side canyon off the Colorado River with a severely twisted ankle before, either.

The sun was so sharp even my eyelids were hot. I had one last drink of water left and miles of rocky canyon between me and my canoe. No one would be expecting me for another week and the raven overhead looked suspiciously like a vulture. I thought again of the man at the gas station who had stared when I told him. "Solo," he kept saying, shaking his head like he had water in his ear.

Two days before I had untied my canoe from the trunk of the huge cottonwood tree on the banks of the Colorado River upstream from Horsethief Canyon and slipped as quietly as a piece of driftwood into the current and downstream. It was early morning. July. The heat was not yet up, and the shadows of the morning were still pooled on the canyon walls like deep, clear water. Alone, with no one in the bow to jabber to about how early I got up or how cold the breakfast was, the silence of the sandstone canyon flowed over me like a gentle wind. I laid the paddle down and listened.

Even in a world in which wilderness has been all but tamed and nearly every corner of the map has been stamped with the imprint of Vibram-soled boots, traveling alone is not yet fully accepted. Mention the word "solo" and you had better be prepared for a lot of strange looks from people like park rangers and anxious mothers, not to mention gas station attendants. It is as if people who travel solo must not have any friends to take along or are just plain missing a few rivets from the old cranial thwarts. It is right up there with the alphabet and the Lord's Prayer: one of the first lessons we learn is never to travel alone. Use the "buddy system" as the *Boy Scouts Handbook* calls it. Solo travel never earned anyone a merit badge.

But attitudes have changed, a little. There are good reasons for traveling solo that have nothing to do with lack of friends—silence, for one.

As the world gets more and more crowded, silence becomes a rare natural resource. Wilderness is, or should be, one of the last strongholds for silence. But with regulations on the Grand Canyon allowing trips of up to 25 people and even some environmental groups sponsoring expeditions that seem more like platoons on maneuver than camping trips, wilderness has turned into a social event—"Support Wildlife: Throw a Party," as the bumpersticker says.

Slipping a boat into the current, alone, in the early morning light is a way to turn back to the basics of the sport, to be quiet enough to hear the heartbeat of the wilderness.

I drifted for nearly an hour without paddling, slipping deeper into Horsethief Canyon and watching a single, silver-grey raincloud riding the sky.

The ability to pass through a landscape as softly as a raincloud is another advantage to solo travel. No need to build those three-story fire rings or flatten vegetation with a dozen tents. The campsite of a solo traveler can look no more disturbed than it would be by a strong wind. The old axiom of "take only pictures, leave only footprints" has been changed. Now, it is "take only pictures." It is easy to leave no footprints when there are only two feet on your trip.

I stopped paddling, bowed slightly forward like the heron on the shore, and drifted to within 10 yards [9 m]. The great blue never moved. Like a porcelain statue it stood motionless, only the light playing in its yellow eyes. I drifted by, never looking back.

Traveling alone it is possible to move quietly and to see more wildlife. And, the lack of someone to share the view with etches it more clearly in your mind, scratching it on the glass of your memory. It strips the barriers between the traveler and the experience.

For hours before stashing my canoe and heading up the side canyon, I sat tracing the pattern some ancient wind had made in the sand, patterns that had been turned to stone in a ruffled rock wall. Traveling alone means traveling at your own pace, another advantage to one as skilled at being sidetracked as I am.

I thought about all this as I lay on my back in the dirt and stared up at the black belly of the circling raven. This was exactly the kind of thing that raises eyebrows when you say you are going solo. "What if you broke an ankle?" I can hear my mother saying. "Yeah, what if?" I think lying there in the dirt.

There has always been an element of challenge in wilderness travel. In a group the challenge is diluted. Solo, the challenges are magnified. They are personal and focused. Perhaps in a world where wilderness has had the edges filed off, traveling solo is a way to reinstate the wildness. People have been traveling solo for thousands of years—hunters, warriors, questers of visions—and one severely sprained ankle shouldn't stand in any-one's way.

I lay there until the darkness fell and the full moon rose. Then, by padding the top of my camera tripod and using it as a crutch, I hobbled back toward the canoe, ankle throbbing, my tongue bloated from dehy-dration. I vowed not to stop at the same gas station on my way home. In the dark, I smiled to myself about the strange outline my single shadow cast against the rock in the moonlight and wondered if the stars made noise as they sailed through the heavens. I stopped to rest and listen, sure that this far out in the wilderness and alone I would hear them if they did.

◆

Insights and Outlooks

1. How do you think travelling solo helped Jeff Rennicke to better understand himself? What, in your opinion, are the advantages of "going alone"? What are the hazards?

2. Have you or has someone you know ever had a "wilderness" experience like the author's, or have you heard about a similar experience? Tell the story.

3. "Traveling solo is a way to reinstate the wildness." What does this comment mean to you?

4. Describe a time in your life when being alone has helped you to learn something about yourself. You may choose to write a poem or a prose passage.

THE SEARCH FOR
THE PERFECT BODY

◆

Mary Walters Riskin

How do the media, particularly television, movies, and magazines, affect our view of the perfect body image?

Too tall!   Too short!   Too fat!   Too thin!   Too clumsy!   Too weak!

Who do we say these negative things about? Not our friends. Not people we respect. Sometimes, maybe, we think or say them about people we don't like. But mostly they're said about ourselves. No matter how good you feel about your abilities and your accomplishments, it's pretty difficult to act confident if you don't feel good about the way you look.

I hate the way I look. —Darlene, 15, a typical teenager.

The present epidemic of self-dislike is related to the whole idea of "body image." Body image is really two images. One stares back at us when we look in the mirror: that's our Actual Body Image. The other is a mental picture of what we think we ought to look like: our Idealized Body Image.

Sometimes the Idealized Body Image is so firmly planted in our minds that it affects our judgement of the actual image in the mirror. We don't see our legs the way they really are—instead we see them compared to "how they ought to look." Instead of saying, "Those are my legs, not bad!" we say, "Those are my legs and they're too fat!" or "That's my nose and it's too big."

Walking away from the mirror, we feel inadequate and miserable. Unhappy with our perceived appearance, we can't relax or feel secure with other people. If you tell yourself over and over, "I'm ugly," you start to believe it and act like it's true. Self-confidence goes right out the window.

I learned the truth at seventeen / that love was meant for beauty queens / and high-school girls with clear-skinned smiles . . .
—Janis Ian, "At Seventeen"

Deep down, we know that there are things much more important than looks. When other people ask us what's important, we say, "Being kind," "Being friendly," or "Being loyal." But when we look in the mirror, we say to ourselves, "What's important is the way I look, and I don't look good enough."

Like our ideas about what's right or what's wrong, or about what's in or out, our ideas about ideal body image come from a number of places . . . starting with our parents and our friends. Even when we're very young, we see adults going on diets, working out, and worrying about the desserts they want to eat. People often apologize before eating, as if they were about to do something immoral. Have you ever made an excuse like, "I didn't eat all day," or "My blood sugar is low" before pigging out?

Kids who are overweight get teased and learn from the experience that bodies are supposed to be thin and muscular, and that there is one perfect body that everyone, especially us, must have.

The image of what that perfect body looks like hits us over and over in the media, particularly in television, movies and magazines. TV programs and advertisements tell us that women should be thin and tall, with a small waist, slender thighs and no hips; while height, large biceps, and strong thighs and quads are desirable in men.

Styles change over the years and this affects what people imagine the ideal body to look like. In the forties and fifties, the pudgy, (by today's standards) Marilyn Monroe look was the style. In the early sixties, everyone wanted to be blond and tanned; the "Beach Boys" look was in. Today, blondes are unhappy because people make jokes about them, and tans are associated with over-age movie stars and with over-exposure to the sun, so the look has changed again.

One glance around school or the shopping mall makes it clear that in the real world people come in every shape, size, age and colour. But after looking at models and actors all day long, the fact that we don't look the way they do makes us feel inadequate.

When I was 18-years-old, and did look perfect, I was so insecure that I would face the wall in elevators because I knew the lighting was bad. —Cybill Shepherd, actress.

We're "too fat" compared to whom? "Too short" compared to whom? Sometimes the perfect body we're looking for doesn't even belong to the person we think it does.

But we continue to diet, exercise and contemplate the cost of plastic surgery, trying to turn ourselves into people we can't be. Some people make themselves exhausted and even sick with starvation diets to lose weight or with drugs to improve their strength, only to discover that no matter what they do, they're still not happy with the way they look.

She ain't pretty, she just looks that way. —The Northern Pikes

With so many unhappy people lacking self-esteem and a positive self-image, sales of hair dyes, make-up, exercise equipment and diet plans are booming. People want to buy these things because they think they'll make them perfect. And perfect is happy. Well, at least the advertisers are happy!

There's some evidence that things are changing. Magazines such as *Sports Illustrated* are actually telling their models to gain a few pounds. Suddenly, the anorexic look is out. Not every character on television has to be perfect anymore, and some TV shows like *Degrassi* have made a genuine effort to portray people the way they really are. Characters from Roseanne to Uncle Buck are breaking down the false physical ideals. But there's still a lot of room for improvement.

If I spent all my life worrying about what I didn't like about myself, I'd never have fun. —Susan, 15

While we're waiting for the media to change, we can change ourselves. Not our bodies, but our attitudes. We can stop playing the Ideal Body Image game in our heads. We can accept that the way we are right now is okay. We look like us, and each one of us is different. When we start to focus on ourselves as individuals, we begin to develop the self-confidence behind the most attractive look of all.

I look like this because I want to. I like looking like this.
—Sinead O'Connor

◆

Insights and Outlooks

1. What did you learn about self-esteem and a positive self-image from reading this article?

2. Where do our ideas about ideal body image come from? List the sources. Which do you think are most influential? Why?

3. In your opinion, how can we change our attitudes so that we aren't constantly comparing ourselves to an ideal body image?

4. View a television program you watch regularly. Analyze how the characters are portrayed. Are they realistic? If not, why not? Are situations true-to-life? How could the show be made more realistic? Present a report on your findings to the class.

A CHILD IN
PRISON CAMP

◆

Shizuye Takashima

Why were Japanese Canadian families kept in internment camps during World War II? Do you think this was just? This is one child's journal account of the experience.

August 1945

We hear the terrifying news. The atomic bomb! Father and mother are silent. Mrs. Kono looks so upset. I go to see Mary. Her mother is crying. There is a terrible tension in the camp. Mr. Mori and the other veterans are openly cursed and threatened. Some blame them for the bomb. No one speaks to Mr. Mori. I saw him this morning. He stared at me. He held his stick very tight to his thin body. I backed away and turned, for I didn't want to pass him. I wondered what he thought as I hurried into the house. I can't understand all this hatred, especially among ourselves. . . .

The End of the War

At last the war with Japan is at an end! We are not surprised, we have been expecting it for months now. It hits the older people very hard. They are given two choices by the Canadian Government: to sign a paper and renounce their Canadian citizenship and return to Japan, or to remain here and be relocated elsewhere. There are terrible quarrels. Those who have signed to return to Japan are called "fools"; the ones who have chosen to stay in Canada are called "dogs," slang for traitors. The Kono family, Mr. Shimizu, our father's friend, all sign to return to Japan. We feel sad that Kay-ko is leaving us. All those families must move to another camp, at Tashme, not far from Vancouver. From there, they will go to Vancouver, then on to Japan.

My mother and I just wait, hoping. Then one day,
out of the blue, father says quietly: "We go east!
I've placed an application. We sign to go to Toronto."
He speaks quietly, more to mother than to me.

"It is useless to return now. My family, God knows
where they are, if any are still alive. I'm glad it's over.
We'll just have to start again. It won't be easy for us."
He looks strange. He rises from his chair quickly
and walks out. I feel sorry for him. The atomic bomb
has upset everyone deeply, too. It seems so wrong.
Mother looks at me, smiles. Her eyes beam.
"See, I told you, I told you, he would see the sense
in remaining here. We can't return to Japan.
They have nothing now, no food, clothes,
houses for their own people. Here, we have each other.
Write to Yuki and David." I write immediately.

Yuki is in Hamilton, Ontario, living with another friend. I am so happy, so
is mother. Father is quiet, but he starts to make boxes with our cousin, Mr.
Fujiwara, the carpenter, to pack our clothes in. Our cousins are remaining
in camps awhile longer, but they, too, have signed to stay in Canada.

Mother and I begin to pack. I have to leave many things
I have grown to love behind. My favorite "dutch shoe"
which Yuki gave me almost two Christmases ago
is still by my bed, on the narrow shelf near the candle.
I pick it up. The candies and nuts are gone.
The sparkly, gold rice is dull,
many grains have already fallen off;
more drop into my hand. But as I hold it
I can still feel the love which the kind Sisters
put into it just when we needed love so much.
I place it back on the shelf. It is too fragile to pack.

September 1945

It is almost three years to the day since we left Vancouver. The papers for
us to leave for the east come through. This is our last week in New Denver.

I go to the lake for the last time with mother
to rinse our clothes. The water is still warm.
I swish the white sheets in the clear water.
Mother is wringing the clothes. She is singing,
she looks so happy. I wonder what David will
look like. I say, "We won't be doing this in Toronto."
Mother sighs, stops, looks at the mountains.
"All in all, Shichan, the three years have not been very hard,

when you think of all the poor people who have been
killed and hurt, and now the suffering in Japan."

Mother and I look out into the distance. A small bird
swoops gracefully down towards the still water.
Another follows. Their pure joy in doing this
is reflected in their flight. The morning mist is slowly
rising from the lake. It looks like it is on fire.
The sun's rays try to seep through the mist.
Everything looks all misty and gray-yellow. I know
I shall remember this beautiful scene,
doing our chores for the last time with nature
all-giving and so silent. Mother bends her frail body,
continues to rinse the clothes. I go back to helping her.
There is warmth between us, and I feel her happiness.

I try to absorb it all, for I know it will be gone soon.
Toronto is a large city. David has written
it is in flat country, by Lake Ontario.
There are no mountains, no snow-capped mountains.

Instead will be concrete buildings, apartments, buses, cars.
But I am looking forward to this, too. Instead of
the sounds of insects and frogs and wild dogs at night,
we will have street sounds, and go to school with
other children, all kinds of children.

Our last night in camp, I go out of the house.
I watch the red rays of the glorious sun.
It spreads its burning arms to the brilliant early autumn
sky, touches the dark pines in the distance.
They catch fire. I hold my breath.
It is aflame, all red for a long time.

Then the rays of the sun slowly begin to fade
behind the now deep purple mountains. The trees,
the mountains all turn into a dark mysterious silhouette as
I stay rooted to the spot. Night comes on.
The pale, pale moon is suspended in the scarlet sky.
I stay standing a long time watching it,
for I want to remember it forever.

◆

Insights and Outlooks

1. Describe the author's attitude to her internment in a camp. Do you think that you would have felt the same way?

2. Despite being in a camp for three years during World War II, what positive and beautiful things did Shizuye Takashima find in the world around her?

3. Canadians come from different cultural, racial, and ethnic backgrounds, but as human beings they nevertheless share common bonds and interests. What does this diary suggest these bonds and interests are?

4. Imagine that you have been put in jail, not because you committed a crime, but because of who you are. Write a diary entry or a poem expressing your feelings.

VOICES OF THE GRANDMOTHERS:
RECLAIMING A METIS HERITAGE
◆

Christine Welsh

"My grandmother was my only living connection with the past, my only hope of finding out who I really was . . ."

This is the story of my search for the voices of my grandmothers. It is not a story which presumes to speak for all native people, for we come from many nations and we have many different stories, many different voices. I can only tell my own story, in my own voice. Leslie Marmon Silko, the Laguna poet and storyteller, puts it this way:

> As with any generation
> the oral tradition depends upon each person
> listening and remembering a portion
> and it is together —
> all of us remembering what we have heard together —
> that creates the whole story
> the long story of the people.
>
> I remember only a small part,
> But this is what I remember.*

I grew up in Saskatchewan, the great-granddaughter of Metis people who, in the late 1860s, migrated west from Red River in pursuit of the last great buffalo herds and eventually settled in the Qu'Appelle Valley of southern Saskatchewan. My great-grandparents were among the first Metis families to set up camp down on the Flats beside Mission Lake where the village of Lebret now stands. As long as the buffalo were plentiful they continued to live from the hunt, wintering in the Cypress Hills and returning to Lebret each summer to sell their buffalo robes, meat and pemmican at the Hudson's Bay Company post at Fort Qu'Appelle. With the disappearance of the buffalo they no longer wintered out on the plains, choosing to remain at Lebret and earn their living by trading, freighting, farming and

---

* Leslie Marmon Silko, *Storyteller* (New York: Seaver Books, 1981): 6-7.

ranching. They are buried there beside the lake among their kinfolk, and the names on the headstones in that little cemetery—Blondeau, Delorme, Desjarlais, Ouellette, Pelletier, Welsh and many more—bear silent witness to the diaspora of the Red River Metis.

I don't know when I first realized that amongst the ghostly relatives there was Indian blood. It was something that just seemed to seep into my consciousness through my pores. I remember my bewilderment when the other children in my predominantly white, middle-class school began to call me "nichi" on the playground. I had never heard the word before and was blissfully ignorant of its meaning, but it wasn't long before I understood that to them it meant "dirty Indian."

By the time I was in high school I had invented an exotic ethnicity to explain my black hair and brown skin and I successfully masqueraded as French or even Hawaiian, depending on who asked. But I still lived in mortal terror that the truth would get out. In 1969, when the province of Saskatchewan dedicated a monument to Louis Riel, all the other girls in my class took advantage of a perfect autumn day and skipped classes to attend the ceremonies. I decided not to go with them and afterward, much to my horror, was commended by the teacher in front of the whole class for behaviour which he deemed to be exemplary—given the fact, he said, that I was the only one who could claim a legitimate right to attend such an observance by virtue of my ancestry. This oblique reference went right over the heads of most of my classmates, but my cheeks still burned with the knowledge that I had been found out. It was no use: no matter how hard I tried to hide it, my native background seemed to be written all over me.

The 1960s gave rise to a new pride in native identity among native people across Canada, and even though I had no contact with other native people, I was swept up by the spirit of the times and began to feel that it was no longer necessary to try to hide who I was. But who was I? By the time I reached university in the early 1970s, denial of my native ancestry had given way to a burning need to know. My curiosity was fuelled by the discovery of a much-worn volume entitled *The Last Buffalo Hunter*, a biography of my great-grandfather, Norbert Welsh, which had been written in the 1930s and rescued by my mother from a second-hand bookshop. I revelled in the references to Norbert's Indian mother and his part-Indian wife, but I didn't really understand that I was reading about a distinctly Metis experience which was separate from that of the Indians— or that it was, in fact, one of the few existing memoirs to be left by a Red River Metis.

Though I was clearly interested in tearing away the shroud of mystery that seemed to surround our native ancestors, my attempts were largely futile. Whenever I tried to raise the subject, strenuous attempts were made, especially by my grandmother, to diminish and deny any connection we might have to native people. She actively discouraged my burgeoning interest in and involvement with "things Indian": "we" were very different from "them," she implied, and such associations would only bring me grief.

Despite my grandmother's dire predictions, I was increasingly drawn to Indian people by my desperate need to find out who I was and where I belonged. Though I made every effort to fit into Indian society I was continually made aware that here, too, I was an outsider—this time because I was too "white." Nevertheless, I spent much of the next fifteen years in "Indian country," travelling to Indian communities across Canada and making documentary films on issues of concern to native people, and eventually the pieces of my identity began to fall into place. . . .

This experience recording native oral history was largely responsible for rekindling my relationship with my own grandmother. This happened quite unexpectedly, because in most of the Indian communities we visited it was the men who were put forward as being the tribal historians, and as a consequence we spent most of our time interviewing men. Yet often, when my husband and I had finished interviewing an old man, his wife would manage to manoeuver me out to the kitchen so that she could speak to me alone. Over cups of strong tea, these women told me the stories of their lives—their experience of marriage and childbirth, their hopes and fears for their children, the work they did, the things that gave them pleasure, and the intricate workings of the communities in which they lived—all freely given, and deliberately so, well after the tape-recorder had been turned off and well out of ear-shot of the men in the next room. For the most part these women were reluctant to be "interviewed" in any formal sense, insisting that they knew nothing about history and that nobody would be interested in what they had to say. But I began to realize that, without their story, an "Indian history of Canada" would be shamefully incomplete, and so I painstakingly went about overcoming their reluctance to speak. In the process I was forced yet again to re-examine my conventional notions of what was historically important and to recognize that the everyday lives of women—the unique patterns and rhythms of female experience—are history, too. In the end, it was this revelation—and the sense of kinship I felt to the native women who shared their life stories with me—that finally led me back to my own grandmother.

I had seen very little of my grandmother during the years I spent in "Indian country." I was living in Toronto, she was in Regina, and our contact consisted of occasional letters and brief visits once or twice a year. But the passage of time and my own changing perceptions of the value of native women's experience gradually led me to see her in a whole new light. Whereas in my youth I had felt nothing but contempt for the values that had led her to deny her native heritage, I now began to feel a genuine bond of compassion and respect for this formidable old lady who seemed to shrink visibly and grow more fragile with each passing season. I was acutely aware that just as we were getting to know each other we would soon be separated for good. She was my only living connection with the past, my only hope of finding out who I really was so, despite her reluctance to talk about the past, I kept on asking my questions. And while she continued to maintain steadfastly the distinctions between our family and other native people, she must have had some sense of how important this was for me because she began to try to give me some answers. We spent hours poring over old family photographs, putting names and faces to those ghostly ancestors who had haunted my childhood. And then, quite suddenly, she died.

My grandmother had very few possessions, but care was taken to distribute what little she had among her children and grandchildren. I received a child's sampler, embroidered by my grandmother's mother in 1890 when she was still a schoolgirl. There, woven into the cloth amongst the crucifixes and barnyard animals, was my great-grandmother's name: Maggie Hogue. Ironically, my grandmother had bequeathed to me that which she had found so difficult to give me while she was alive—the key to unlocking the mystery of who I was.

We had finished our fieldwork for the "Indian History of Canada," so I decided to pursue my deepening interest in native women's history by studying the work done by Sylvia Van Kirk on the role of native women in the North American fur-trade. I learned that, initially, very few white women were permitted to brave the perils of the "Indian country" so most fur-traders took Indian and mixed-blood women as "country wives." These "marriages à la façon du pays" were socially sanctioned unions, even though they were not formalized according to the laws of church or state. But with the establishment of the Red River settlement white women began to go west, and it soon became fashionable for the traders to legally marry white women and to try to sever their ties with their native country wives.

17

In the forefront of this trend was Sir George Simpson, governor of Rupert's Land and, by all accounts, the most important personage in the Canadian fur-trade, who had taken as his country wife a mixed-blood woman named Margaret Taylor. Though she bore him two sons, Margaret Taylor was abandoned by Simpson when he married his English cousin, a move which signalled the widespread rejection of native women as marriage partners by "men of station" in fur-trade society and reflected the increasing racial and social prejudice against native women throughout pre-Confederation Canada. Clearly, Margaret Taylor's story epitomized a crucial chapter in the history of native women in Canada, but I was equally intrigued by its epilogue—her hastily arranged marriage to a French-Canadian voyageur whose name was startlingly familiar: Amable Hogue.

On the basis of my great-grandmother's faded sampler and a rather incidental footnote in a history book, I began a search that eventually verified my connection to my great-great-great-grandmother, Margaret Taylor. For me it was the beginning of a journey of self-discovery—of unravelling the thick web of denial, shame, bitterness and silence that had obscured my past and picking up the fragile threads that extended back across time, connecting me to the grandmothers I had never known and to a larger collective experience that is uniquely and undeniably Metis.

My search for my grandmothers was hampered both by the inadequacies of traditional historical sources with respect to women and by the code of silence that existed in my own family with respect to our native heritage. But, after venturing down a couple of blind alleys, I finally called my great-aunt Jeanne, who is my grandmother's youngest sister and the only surviving female relative on that side of my family. When I called Grandma Jeanne I hadn't seen or spoken to her in more than twenty years, yet she was surprised and touched that I remembered her and seemed eager to help me in any way she could. Grandma Jeanne knew about Margaret Taylor, and knew that she had some connection to George Simpson, but said that this had never been discussed because, in the words of Jeanne's mother, it had brought shame on the family. Nonetheless, Grandma Jeanne was able to tell me the names of Margaret Taylor's daughters and granddaughters, and in the act of naming them I finally had the sense of reaching back and grasping hands with all my grandmothers and great-grandmothers—right back to Margaret Taylor. . . .

My great-great-great-grandmother was just twenty-one years old when she became the "country wife" of the Governor of Rupert's Land. Though George Simpson was notorious for indulging in short-lived liaisons with young native women, his relationship with Margaret Taylor appeared to be different. He relied on her companionship to an unusual degree, insisting that she accompany him on his historic cross-continental canoe journey from Hudson Bay to the Pacific in 1828. Not only did Simpson recognize and assume responsibility for their two sons, but he also provided financial support for Margaret's mother and referred to Thomas Taylor as his brother-in-law, thus giving Margaret and the rest of fur-trade society every reason to believe that their relationship constituted a legitimate "country marriage." Nevertheless, while on furlough in England in 1830—and with Margaret and their two sons anxiously awaiting his return at Fort Alexander—Simpson married his English cousin, Frances Simpson.

It is not hard to imagine Margaret's shock when she learned that the Governor was returning with a new wife. No doubt she and her children were kept well out of sight when Simpson and his new bride stopped at Fort Alexander during their triumphant journey from Lachine to Red River. Once the Simpsons were installed at Red River the Governor lost no time in arranging for Margaret's "disposal," a few months later she was married to Amable Hogue. . . .

Amable Hogue, who had been among Simpson's elite crew of voyageurs, was hired as a stonemason on the construction of Simpson's new headquarters at Lower Fort Garry. From her vantage point in the Metis labourers' camp just outside the walls, Margaret would have been able to watch the Governor and his bride take up residence in their magnificent new home. For his service, the Hudson's Bay Company gave Hogue a riverfront lot on the Assiniboine River just west of the Forks, and it was there on the banks of the Assiniboine River that Margaret Taylor and her daughters and granddaughters spent most of the rest of their lives, raising their families and working beside their men-folk on the buffalo hunts and riverfront farms that were the mainstay of the Red River Metis. . . .

It is impossible to know when the process of denial and assimilation began in my own family, but I feel in my heart that it goes right back to what happened to Margaret Taylor. Here, I believe, are the roots of our denial—denial of that fact of blood that was the cause of so much pain and suffering and uncertainty about the future. Is it such a surprise that, many years later, Margaret's own son would choose to describe his mother as "a sturdy Scotswoman" rather than the halfbreed that she really was? Perhaps Margaret herself perpetrated this myth, if not for her son's sake then certainly for her daughters', to try to spare them a fate similar to her own and that of her mother. I'll never know. But I do know that the denial of our native heritage, which has been passed on from generation to generation of my family, is explicable in light of those events that took place so long ago, and I am finally able to see it not as a betrayal but as the survival mechanism that it most certainly was. For we *did* survive—even though, for a time, we were cut off from our past and our people—and we did so largely because of the resourcefulness, adaptability and courage of my grandmothers.

◆

Insights and Outlooks

1. What prompted Christine Welsh to "search for the voices" of her grandmothers? Have you or has anyone you know had a similar need to uncover their past? Discuss why you might be curious about your ancestors and what you could discover.

2. How do you feel about Christine Welsh's need to hide her native heritage and about how the native "country wives" of the early fur-traders were treated in Canada?

3. Do you agree with Christine Welsh's explanation that the denial of her native heritage from generation to generation was a survival mechanism rather than a betrayal? Explain.

4. Describe something about your own heritage which you have discovered from listening to the "voices" of some member of your family or through some other means. How has this helped you to discover who you are?

CLOSE TIES

**It is only important to love the world . . .
to regard the world and ourselves and all beings
with love, admiration, and respect.**
Hermann Hesse

Who are you closest to? What do you think makes you feel close to these people—your friends, family, care-givers, or others? Is the relationship always stable, or is it sometimes stormy and changing? Is it always easy to talk about your deepest feelings with the people closest to you? Close relationships are one of the great mysteries of our lives. They can surprise us, delight us, make us angry or sad—and we can't always explain why. But most of us would agree that somehow relationships are wonderfully rewarding. They can teach us a great deal about ourselves and others if we make the effort to discover what they have to offer.

TRAVELER

Garrison Keillor

"The night when your child returns with dust on his shoes from a country you've never seen is a night you would gladly prolong into a week."

My fifteen-year-old son has just returned from abroad with a dozen rolls of exposed film and a hundred dollars in uncashed travelers' checks, and is asleep at the moment, drifting slowly westward toward Central Time. His blue duffel bag lies on the hall floor where he dropped it, about four short strides into the house. Last night, he slept in Paris, and the twenty nights before that in various beds in England and Scotland, but evidently he postponed as much sleep as he could: when he walked in and we embraced and he said he'd missed home, his electrical system suddenly switched off, and he headed half-unconscious for the sack, where I imagine he may beat his old record of sixteen hours.

I don't think I'll sleep for a while. This household has been running a low fever over the trip since weeks before it began, when we said, "In one month, you'll be in London! Imagine!" It was his first trip overseas, so we pressed travel books on him, and a tape cassette of useful French phrases; drew up a list of people to visit; advised him on clothing and other things. At the luggage store where we went to buy him a suitcase, he looked at a few suitcases and headed for the duffels and knapsacks. He said that suitcases were more for old people. I am only in my forties, however, and I pointed out that a suitcase keeps your clothes neater—a sports coat, for example. He said he wasn't taking a sports coat. The voice of my mother spoke through me. "Don't you want to look nice?" I said. He winced in pain and turned away.

My mother and father and a nephew went with him on the trip, during which he called home three times: from London, from Paris, and from a village named Ullapool, in the Highlands. "It's like no place in America," he reported from London. Near Ullapool, he hiked through a crowd of Scottish sheep and climbed a mountain in a rainstorm that almost blew him off the summit. He took cover behind a boulder, and the sun came out. In the village, a man spoke to him in Gaelic, and, too polite to interrupt, my son listened to him for ten or fifteen minutes, trying to nod and murmur in the right places. The French he learned from the cassette didn't hold water in Paris—not even his fallback phrase, *"Parlez-vous anglais?"* The French he said it to shrugged and walked on. In Paris, he bought a hamburger at a tiny shop run by a Greek couple, who offered Thousand Island dressing in place of ketchup. He described Notre Dame to me, and the Eiffel Tower, as he had described Edinburgh, Blair Castle, hotel rooms, meals, people he saw on the streets.

"What is it like?" I asked over and over. I myself have never been outside the United States, except twice when I was in Canada. When I was eighteen, a friend and I made a list of experiences we intended to have before we reached twenty-one, which included hopping a freight to the West Coast, learning to play the guitar, and going to Europe. I've done none of them. When my son called, I sat down at the kitchen table and leaned forward and hung on every word. His voice came through clearly, though two of the calls were like ship-to-shore radio communication in which you have to switch from Receive to Send, and when I interrupted him with a "Great!" or a "Really?" I knocked a little hole in his transmission. So I just sat and listened. I have never listened to a telephone so intently and with so much pleasure as I did those three times. It was wonderful and moving to hear news from him that was so new to me. In my book, he was the first man to land on the moon, and I knew that I had no advice to give him and that what I had already given was probably not much help.

The unused checks that he's left on the hall table—almost half the wad I sent him off with—is certainly evidence of that. Youth travels light. No suitcase, no sports coat, not much language, and a slim expense account, and yet he went to the scene, got the story, and came back home safely. I sit here amazed. The night when your child returns with dust on his shoes from a country you've never seen is a night you would gladly prolong into a week.

◆
————————

Insights and Outlooks

1. Find a sentence you think reveals what the father has learned from his son's travels. Write about what you think the sentence shows.

2. What is the longest period of time you have ever spent away from your family or friends? Were things different when you came back? How? Did they stay different?

3. Ask one of your parents or an adult you know well to read this piece. Ask them what it made them think about or what surprised them. Share your thoughts and ideas about the piece with them. Then write a short summary of the adult's main response and discuss it with the class or in a smaller group.

4. Rewrite "Traveler" from the son's (or daughter's) perspective. What would he or she be thinking about the father's helpful suggestions and during the phone calls home?

MY MOTHER,
MY RIVAL

◆

Mariah Burton Nelson

**"What better way to get to know someone than to test your abilities
together, to be daring and sweaty and exhausted together?"**

The first time my mother and I competed against each other she was 37;
I was five. We swam one lap of our neighbor's pool. She won.

As a five-year-old I didn't realize—and I don't think my mother realized
—that she was teaching me about love. We thought we were just fooling
around.

Later we had diving competitions, which she also won, though I would
argue, and she would concede, that I deserved higher marks for versatil-
ity. For my jackknife, I would *boing* into the air, desperately grab my toes,
then splash down on all fours. For my back dive, I would reach my hands
meekly overhead, then fall into the water as if I'd been shot. Mom had
only one dive—the swan dive—but if you do only one dive you can learn
to do it very well. She'd fly skyward, arch like a ship's proud figurehead,
then streamline toward the water and quietly, tapered toes last, disappear.

Eventually I gave up diving—pointing my toes always seemed so unnat-
ural—but I joined a swim team, and by the time I was 10, I could outswim
Mom. ("Oh, I don't know about that," responds my mother now. "I think
you were eleven.")

Mom was my fan, too, when I would race against Betty and Letty
Landers, the indomitable twins at Cedarbrook Country Club in our mini-
town of Blue Bell, Pennsylvania. Betty had skinny arms as sharp and swift
as Osterizer blades; Letty had furious legs that started kicking mid-racing
dive, like a windup bathtub toy. I didn't stand a chance.

But Mom would root for me anyway, yelling from the sidelines as if I
could hear her underwater. She'd transport my friends and me to swimming meets all over the county (she liked to drive fast over the hilly, back-
country roads so we'd fly up out of our seats and scream), and she even
arranged practice time for me during family vacations to the New Jersey
shore. It made me feel important to skip deep-sea fishing trips with my
dad and siblings to work out at a pool.

Mom was also my teammate: the two of us ganged up on the Landers twins in the mother-daughter relay races at Cedarbrook's year-end championships. Mrs. Landers, a lounge lizard of sorts, had a great tan but no speed, so Mom and I were undefeated for six years until adolescence caught up with me and I left swimming for more important things, like basketball.

So when I think about competition I also remember the Landers twins, who would join me in the showers after the meets, the three of us giggling and whispering until all the hot water ran out. I think about Gordon, whom I later met on a basketball court; he would guard me by pushing on my waist with one hand and I still remember that push, and how much more honest it felt than my boyfriends' gropings. I remember six-foot-three-inch Heidi, my teammate, who would rebound the ball viciously, sharp elbows out; I hated her elbows but loved her audacity and her long strong hands, mirrors of my own. When I think about competition I realize that beginning with my fiercely, playfully competitive mother—who at 55 took up tennis and at 60 tried downhill skiing—athletes have taught me most of what I know about love.

Competition is about passion for perfection, and passion for other people who join in this impossible quest. What better way to get to know someone than to test your abilities together, to be daring and sweaty and exhausted together?

"If you compare yourself with others," a line in the inspirational prose poem "Desiderata" warns, "you may become vain and bitter, for always there will be greater and lesser persons than yourself." Yet I find that by comparing myself to other athletes, I become both self-confident and humble. Through competition, I have learned to acknowledge my failures and make allowances for the failures of others. Isn't that what intimacy is about?

But competition is not all fun and games. Like families, competitors can bring out the worst as well as the best in each other. Like romance, competition has many faces, some of them ugly. In addition to showing me my grace and graciousness, the mirror of sports has reflected back to me my jealousy, pettiness, and arrogance.

For instance: I have taken a friend to a tennis court, said, "Let's just hit a few," then fired the ball down her throat. I have, during a recreational, two-on-two volleyball game, refused to pass to my partner so that we could win.

Believing that "competitive" was a dirty word, I used to say, "I'm not competitive, I just happen to be the best." My teammate Heidi and I had a tearful yelling match one night after a basketball game, and I accused her of not passing me the ball. "How am I supposed to score more than 19 points if you won't even look in my direction?" I screamed. "Why are you so competitive with me?"

"Look who's being competitive!" she countered. "Since when is 19 points something to be ashamed of? Only when it's compared to my 29, right?"

Later I told friends, "I've realized that I am in fact very competitive."

"No!" they said sarcastically. "You?"

I guess I was the last to notice.

But despite such humiliations, Heidi and I are good friends, and because we have played basketball together, she knows me better than friends who only chat with me over lunch. I am never more naked than in the heat of competition. I never feel more vulnerable than after flubbing a catch in the ninth inning, or rolling a bowling ball into the gutter.

In sports, as in love, one can never pretend.

It is for this reason that some women avoid sports altogether; they choose not to unveil themselves in that way. In a society in which women's attractiveness is of utmost importance, why get muddy and sweaty and exhausted? Why risk anger, frustration, aggression, and other unseemly emotions? It is far safer to stay seated demurely in a café.

"I hate competition!" some friends have said to me. These are the women who were never taught how to throw or catch a ball and I don't blame them. As an untrained musician, I know that if my childhood had been filled with music competitions, and I were chosen last for music teams and humiliated in front of other great musicians, I would resent both music and competition. Who enjoys doing things poorly?

A third reason many women have an ambivalent, if not downright hostile attitude toward sports—and why others embrace sports—is that team sports are an intense, physical activity. To play sports with women is to love women, to be passionate about women, to be intimate with women. How scary. Or, depending on your point of view, how thrilling.

So competition is about love, I noticed early, and, I noticed later, about fear. That's why I like to remember my childhood, when the love part was relatively pure, untainted by fear or failure, fear of looking like a fool, or fear of loving women. I feel blessed to have had a big brother who taught me how to throw, and a mother who never let me win. Even today, when I compete at water polo, bad-knee tennis, Nerf basketball, Ping-Pong, billiards—whatever I can persuade someone else to play with me—my favorite competitor is my mom. She is 63 now, I am 31, and when I visit her in Phoenix, we still race. "Give me a head start," she'll suggest, "or better yet, I'll do freestyle and you swim backstroke, just kicking, okay?"

If she wins, she smacks her hand against the wall, jerks her head up, and yells, "Ha! Beat you!"

I complain that she must have cheated. She splashes me. I dunk her. We laugh a lot. And I think, yes, this must be love.

◆

Insights and Outlooks

1. In this article, the author says, "Through competition, I have learned to acknowledge my failures and make allowances for the failures of others. Isn't that what intimacy is about?" How do you feel about competition? Does your experience coincide with the author's?

2. What role do you think competition played in the relationship between the author and her mother and the author and her friends? Are you competitive with family or friends? What part, if any, does it play in your relationship with others close to you?

3. Do you think it is true that when you engage in an intense activity with other people, such as competitive sports, other games, or even a trip, that people "unveil" themselves? Discuss.

4. Write an account of a competitive situation you were involved in. Describe your feelings, how others responded, and how it affected your relationship with others.

LOVE AND MARRIAGE

◆

Bill Cosby

**"The first time I saw her, she was crossing the street
to the school yard and for one golden moment our eyes met."**

I can't remember where I have left my glasses, but I can still remember the
smell of the first girl I ever fell in love with when I was twelve: a blend of
Dixie Peach pomade on her hair and Pond's cold cream on her skin;
together they were honeysuckle for me. And just as heady as her scent
was the thought that I was in love with the only girl in the world for me
and would marry her and take care of her forever in a palace in North
Philadelphia. Because I wanted to make a wondrous impression on this
girl, grooming was suddenly important to me. Before puberty, happiness
in appearance for me was pants that didn't fall down and a football that
stayed pumped; but now I started taking three long baths a day and
washing my own belt until it was white and shining my shoes until I could
see in them a face that was ready for romance.

The first time I saw her, she was crossing the street to the school yard and
for one golden moment our eyes met. Well, maybe the moment was
closer to bronze because she made no response. But at least she had seen
me, just about the way that she saw lampposts, hydrants, and manholes.
Or was there something more? I began to dream; and later that day, when
I was playing with the boys in the yard, it seemed that she was looking at
me and the world was suddenly a better place, especially Twelfth and
Girard.

However, we still never talked, but just traded silent unsmiling looks
whenever we passed. For several days, just her look was enough of a lift
for me; but a higher altitude was coming, for one night at a party, we met
and I actually danced with her. Now I was certain that I was in love and
was going to win her.

I began my conquest with a combination of sporting skill and hygiene: I
made my jump shots and my baths as dazzling as they could be. Oddly
enough, however, although I saw her every day at school and on the

29

weekends too, I never spoke to her. I had what was considered one of the faster mouths in Philadelphia, but I still wasn't ready to talk to her because I feared rejection. I feared:

COSBY: I like you very much. Will you be my girlfriend?
GODDESS: (*Doing a poor job of suppressing a laugh*) I'd rather have some cavities filled.

All I did, therefore, was adore her in silent cleanliness. Each Sunday night, I took a bath and then prepared my shirt and pants for display to her. On Monday morning, I took another bath (Bill the Baptist, I should have been called) and then brushed my hair, my shoes, and my eyelashes and went outside to await the pang of another silent passage.

At last, deciding that I could no longer live this way, I sat down on Sunday night and wrote a note that was almost to her. It was to her constant girlfriend and it said:

Please don't tell her, but find out what she thinks of me.
Bill

The following morning, I slipped the note to the girlfriend and began the longest wait of my life.

Two agonizing days later, the girlfriend slipped me an answer, but I put it into my pocket unread. For hours, I carried it around, afraid to read it because I didn't happen to be in the mood for crushing rejection that day. At last, however, I summoned the courage to open the note and read:

She thinks you're cute.

Not even malaria could have taken my temperature to where it went. I had been called many things, but cute was never one of them.

An even lovelier fever lay ahead, for the next time I saw her, she smiled at me, I smiled at her, and then I composed my next winged message to her friend:

I think she's cute too. Does she ever talk about me?

The answer to this one came return mail and it sounded like something by Keats:

She talks about you a lot. She knows it when you come around her.

And the angels sang! Imagine: she actually *knew* it when I came around her! The fact that she also knew it when gnats came around her in no way dampened my ecstasy.

And so, we continued to smile as we passed, while I planned my next move. My Western Union style had clearly been charming the pants off her (so to speak) and now I launched my most courageous question yet:

Does she have a boyfriend?

When I opened the answer the next day in school, the air left me faster than it left the *Hindenburg*:

Yes.

Trying to recover from this deflation, I told myself that I was still cute. I was the cutest man in second place. But perhaps my beloved wasn't aware of the glory she kept passing by. Once more, I sat down and wrote:

How much longer do you think she'll be going with him? And when she's finished with him, can I be next?

Note the elegance and dignity of my appeal. My dignity, however, did have some trouble with the reply:

She thinks she's going to break up with him in about a week, but she promised Sidney she would go with him next.

Suddenly, my aching heart found itself at the end of a line. But it was like a line at a bank: I knew it was leading to a payoff. I also knew that I could cream Sidney in cuteness.

Once she had made the transition to Sidney, I patiently began waiting for her to get sick of him. I had to be careful not to rush the illness because Sidney belonged to a tough gang and there was a chance that I might not be walking around too well when the time came for me to inherit her.

And then, one magnificent morning, I received the magic words:

She would like to talk to you.

I wrote back to see if she would wait until I had finished my duty at my post as a school crossing guard. Yes, she would wait; I could walk her home. We were going steady now; and how much more torrid our passion would be when I began to *talk* to her.

At last, the words came and I chose them with care. As I walked her home from school, I reached into my reservoir of romantic thoughts, smiled at her soulfully, and said, "How you doing?"

Her response was equally poetic: "All right."

"So we're going steady now?"

"You want to?"

"Yeah. Give me your books."

And now, as if our relationship were not already in the depths of desire, I plunged even deeper by saying, "You wanna go to a movie on Saturday?"

"Why not?"

There might have been reasons. Some people were looking at us now because she was so beautiful, people possibly wondering what she was doing with me; but I knew that I was someone special to be the love of a vision like this, no matter how nearsighted that vision might be.

When we reached her door, I said, "Well, I'll see you Saturday."

"Right," she replied as only she could say it.

"What time?"

"One o'clock."

When this day of days finally arrived, I took her to a theater where I think the admission was a dime. As we took our seats for the matinee, two basic thoughts were in my mind: not to sit in gum and to be a gentleman.

Therefore, I didn't hold her hand. Instead, I put my arm around the top of her seat in what I felt was a smooth opening move. Unfortunately, it was less a move toward love than toward gangrene: with my blood moving uphill, my arm first began to tingle and then to ache. I could not, however, take the arm down and let my blood keep flowing because such a lowering would mean I didn't love her; so I left it up there, its muscles full of pain, its fingertips full of needlepoints.

Suddenly, this romantic agony was enriched by a less romantic one: I had to go to the bathroom. Needless to say, I couldn't let her know about this urge, for great lovers never did such things. The answer to "Romeo, Romeo, wherefore art thou, Romeo?" was not "In the men's room, Julie."

What a prince of passion I was at this moment: my arm was dead, my bladder was full, and I was out of money too; but I desperately needed an excuse to move, so I said, "You want some popcorn?"

"No," she said.

"Fine, I'll go get some."

When I tried to move, every part of me could move except my arm: it was dead. I reached over and pulled it down with the other one, trying to be as casual as a man could be when pulling one of his arms with the other one.

"What's the matter?" she said.

"Oh, nothing," I replied. "I'm just taking both of my arms with me."

A few minutes later, as I came out of the bathroom, I was startled to meet her: she was coming from the bathroom *too*. How good it was to find another thing that we had in common. With empty bladders and full hearts, we returned to our seats to continue our love.

◆

Insights and Outlooks

1. What expectations did Bill Cosby believe he had to fulfill to be attractive to his "first love"? Why do you think he had these expectations? What do you think about them?

2. What feelings did Bill Cosby experience? How did "being in love" change his behaviour? Can you identify with him? How and why?

3. What do you think of Bill Cosby's writing style? Did you find the piece funny? What techniques, words, or phrases do you think add humour?

4. Write a piece about one of your experiences with being in love for the first time. It might be the truth thinly veiled by exaggeration and with name changes . . . or it might be totally fictitious. You could model your piece after Cosby's.

TALES OF A
MOTHER/CONFESSOR

◆

Judy Blume

**Thousands of teens write to Judy Blume
to share their secrets and ask her advice.
But what was her experience with her own family?**

My own adolescent rebellion came late. Somewhere around the age of 35. I don't recommend waiting till then. Better to drag your parents through it than your kids. I was a *good* child in our family. My job was to be happy, to make up for my brother, who wasn't. Even as a teen, I gave my parents little trouble. I told them only what I thought they wanted to hear. I kept the rest to myself. I played my role well, but it took its toll. My rashes were famous all over town. My aunt called me Camille.

Yet my friends envied me. Our house was a haven, a gathering place. Rules were simple and reasonable. My mother was always available (a physical presence if not an emotional one) and my father was warm, funny, loving. He told me if I ever had problems, I should come to him. Other young people did. They'd go to his office just to talk. My father wasn't a psychiatrist or counselor—he was a dentist—yet people of all ages confided in him. But not me. I was his daughter! I wasn't supposed to have problems. (At least that's what I thought.) And I didn't want to disappoint him.

My father died suddenly, when I was 21, and my life changed overnight. We never had the chance to know each other as adults. Until I began to write this piece it never occurred to me that I have taken my father's place, becoming a confidante to thousands of young people who write to me every year, in response to my books.

They write about their most immediate concerns—family, friends, love, loss, sex, school. The same concerns I had as a teenager. They wish their parents would acknowledge their feelings and take them seriously. They wish for unconditional love.

They worry about their parents' problems with drug and alcohol abuse. They are angry, hurt, sad and fearful when their parents divorce. They are hostile to unrealistic expectations for stepfamilies. They will *not* live happily ever after—at least not right away.

They wish their parents would make more time for them.

Sometimes they say how lucky they feel. This usually means a close, loving relationship with parents, siblings and friends. Not a perfect life, but these kids can roll with the punches.

What *has* changed are the numbers of letters about family violence, incest and other abuses. There are letters expressing such hopelessness and despair they leave me in tears. Letters about wanting to die to end the pain.

While most letters are not so pessimistic, these deeply troubled kids need something to believe in—a future with possibilities. Someone has to prove to them that change is possible. Not an easy task. All I can do is offer support and encouragement. I know for the most part they are desperate for someone to listen. As one 16-year-old wrote: "I just want someone to hold me and tell me it's going to be all right."

So I certainly should have been prepared for my own children's adolescence. My daughter and son (and later, my stepdaughter) grew up hearing how lucky they were. "Your mother is Judy Blume. You can tell her anything . . . right?" Wrong. I hoped they would feel they could. But when the going got tough my daughter went to someone else. "My mother just wants to hear that everything is great!" Randy said. Was that true? Had I sent my kids the same message my parents sent to me? I don't know. But if that's the way she perceived it, the rest doesn't matter.

At 16, my sweet daughter became angry, sullen, judgmental, emotionally closed to me. In other words, a typical adolescent. And even though I knew her rejection was necessary to prove she could survive without me, it hurt!

I was feeling very fragile myself at the time, in the midst of my own late adolescence—confused about life, about where I belonged, trying to make up for what I had missed out on when I was young. Two years earlier I had run away from the authority figures in my life—my mother, who I believed had almost total control over me, and my husband. I wanted what every teen wants—to make my own decisions, to control my own life. But the last thing my daughter needed was a parent in the same boat.

My son, Larry, who is two years younger than Randy, wasn't sympathetic to his sister's behavior. He swore he would never act so stupid. Ha! Two years later it was his turn, and he made Randy's rebellion seem tame.

The details of their adolescence belong to them. All I can tell you is what it was like for me. I felt alone and frightened. Like so many recently divorced parents, I blamed myself.

How could this be happening? I wondered. After all, thousands of kids were writing to me every month. They trusted me. I knew how to listen without judging. (Yes, but it's so much easier when they're not *your* kids. And it's so much easier for them to tell someone other than *their* parents.)

Maybe I should have cheered Randy's and Larry's rebellions. At least they came at the right time of life. Years later, when we could talk about what we now refer to as the *difficult* years, Randy said, "You know, Mother, we took turns. We never gave you more trouble than you could handle!"

The good news is, most of us survive our children's adolescent years. My only advice is to stay aware, listen carefully and yell for help if you need it. Somehow, with common sense and humor most of us manage to muddle through. And on the other side is a reward. A new relationship with adult children. I spent last weekend visiting my married daughter at her new home. We laughed a lot and talked about each other's writing projects. It was a lovely weekend. It was worth every minute of her 16th year.

---◆---

Insights and Outlooks

1. Judy Blume speaks of her rebellious stage as coming much later than most. Would you agree that most teens go through a rebellious stage? What are your thoughts and experiences?

2. "Your mother is Judy Blume. You can tell her anything . . . right? Wrong." What feelings do you think Judy Blume is expressing in this statement? Do you find it easier to talk to a "dispassionate listener," someone at a distance, than to someone close to you? Why do you think this might be so?

3. Has your relationship with your parent(s) or care-giver(s) changed since you entered adolescence? How? How do you see this relationship changing in five years? After you leave home? Suggest reasons for any changes.

4. Some people speak of adolescence as a period when normally reasonable people become unreasonable, irrational, moody, rebellious, and downright hard to get along with. Do some reading on the teen years (articles, biographies, autobiographies, fiction) and then debate this statement.

BETWEEN OURSELVES: LETTERS
BETWEEN MOTHERS AND DAUGHTERS
———◆———

**"I have never written a letter like this before
in my short life."**

Dear Mummy: *June 1981*
This last trip to India with you has brought home to me a few hard facts—
facts that I wanted to avoid seeing for some time. As you well know, you
and I have had a few arguments and several days of tensions during the
trip. As I approach my seventeenth year I suddenly ask myself where do I
belong. I know this is the usual teen-age identity crisis, etc., etc. You came
to this country when you were slightly older than I am and married my
father and admired the American lifestyle and tried to be an American as
much as you could. I am born of you who is Indian and my father who is
American. Of course, I am American. Except for a few trips to India I have
little to do with India outwardly. But, I feel how much you would like me to
become Indian sometimes. I cannot explain it with examples. But I feel it
in my bones. The India that you never quite shook off your system comes
back to you now and you want to see your daughter live it, at least partly.

Yes, mummy I know I am wrapped up in many superficial things, things
my friends and peers indulge in and I can understand your need to protect
me. But, I am part of them and in order for me to be accepted by my
friends sometimes I do things which do not always please me either. I
need their approval and I want to be like them sometimes. But, your good
intentions to teach me those good Indian things then clash. Although I
dislike the superficiality of my friends, I cannot move back to your lifestyle just because it is better (for you) or more ancient or deep. Let me live
the life I am surrounded by and reject and suffer as I wish and as many of
my friends are going through . . .

While I understand your point, I must admit sometimes I really do not
know how to communicate to you what I really feel. Words seem to fail on
both sides. That's why I am writing this letter. Perhaps it will be a bit easier.
Dad does not seem to be the problem in this regard. When I argue with
him or reject something he wants me to do, I do not feel such ambivalence

as I do when the same thing happens with you. Isn't it strange! Perhaps, I am a bit Indian under my skin after all. Although every time I visit India after the first two weeks of love and food, I begin to weary of all the slow sloth and all the rest. I ache to come back to my superficial friends with whom I do not always need to use even language. It's the communication that I feel is at stake between you and me and between India and me. Mummy, you did not have to grow up in America; you grew up in India and could keep a lot of nostalgia and good memories when you decided to reject India. When you criticize me, you never think that we were born in two different worlds and that makes a big difference between us even though I am your flesh and blood as you often point out, rightly.

My dearest mother, I cannot be protected by you. Forgive me if I remind you of something you related to me many times. You could not be protected by my grandparents (your parents) when you decided to embrace this culture along with my father. Nor can you protect me despite the fact that we are not separated by physical distance. Perhaps, we are separated by something else and I suspect, that is India.

I have never written a letter like this before in my short life. I feel good about writing this and I would like to hear what you have to say. Ma, perhaps, you and I still can be friends in this way that you and your mother could not be. Let's try. I love you.

Yours,
Rita

---◆---

Insights and Outlooks

1. Rita feels that she and her mother "were born in two different worlds." What do you think she means? What differences do you see between Rita and her mother?
2. Why do people write letters? Why did Rita write this letter? What differences can you see between communicating directly and communicating "at a distance" through a letter?
3. Do you think Rita's letter expresses the problems of the generation gap? What are your experiences? Are your values different from those of the adults closest to you? How and why?
4. Write a letter to someone close to you. Discuss an issue you might normally not feel comfortable talking about. How do you feel after writing the letter?

—— ♦ ◇ ♦ ——

ISSUES AND INSIGHTS

**It is one of the most beautiful
compensations of this life
that no man can sincerely try to
help another without helping himself.**
Ralph Waldo Emerson

Are there issues or problems you worry about?
Drug abuse? Crime? Education? How does each
of us decide what is right or wrong in a society
that constantly bombards us with confusing and
conflicting messages? Whom do we listen to?
Our parents? Our peers? The media? How does
education help? There is much to discover
about ourselves by listening to the experiences
of others who have made their choices.

DEGRASSI TALKS...
ALCOHOL
◆
Teresa's Story

What could make a teenager turn to alcohol?
How big a problem is teenage alcoholism?

Teresa was 12 years old when she started to drink. She became an alcoholic and drank steadily for four years. She is now 18 and has been clean for almost two years. A few years ago, her mom and dad split up and Teresa lives with her dad on a farm where she goes to school and rides her horse.

How did it all begin?
I started drinking because I really didn't feel good about myself. I felt that nobody liked me. I felt very unloved. I felt responsible for everybody else's problems.

Alcohol gave me a false sense of confidence—I could take on the whole world; everything was fine, my family was great, nothing wrong. I could be friendly and alcohol just made me—I thought it made me—feel good. And I thought that nothing else could make me feel that way.

I'm not really sure why I didn't like myself. I guess it was partly a false belief I had that the whole world depended on me and I felt like I was letting the whole world down. I was letting my parents down. I was letting myself down. I'm not really sure what made me think that, but I did.

My mother drank quite a bit. She had a problem with it and when my dad left, I felt that I had to be more responsible. I had to be perfect. I became quite a perfectionist. My marks always had to be perfect. If I got an 86, I wanted an 88.

I also felt that I had to take care of my mother—a sort of reversal of roles. I think that kind of happens with any divorced family but when there's a drinking problem as well, it made me feel very responsible.

I don't really remember my first drink. I've always been around alcohol and I'd just pick up a glass and take a drink. So I could have been 3 when I had my first drink.

That's the way it was in my family. We were always around alcohol and I just started drinking early—around age 12. I was in grade seven.

Becoming an alcoholic

When I was 12, I wasn't really drinking to get drunk. I'd just have a drink to relax me or something like that. But as I got older, I had to drink a lot more to get that feeling of relaxation. When I was 12, one drink would do it, but once I got to be about 14 or 15, I'd have to have a couple more, and by the time I stopped drinking, I was having up to seven drinks a day.

I was very good at hiding that I was drunk. I would just be more outgoing, more friendly. And I wasn't staggering all over the place. When I was drinking, I would drink before I'd go to school so I knew I had to control myself, otherwise I'd get caught.

At the end, my school marks went down quite a bit. I was close to flunking out but after I pulled them back up again.

My friends noticed what was going on but they didn't really want to do anything. I don't know whether it was that they didn't care or what, but they didn't really say anything. They were worried but I don't think they really knew what to do.

When I got into Grade 9, I started drinking before school. Once I was in Grade 10, I felt that I had to have that drink before I could do well in school. Everything revolved around alcohol.

I'd mix something with my orange juice or I'd have a coke in the morning with a bit of rum in it and off I'd go.

At the end, I started taking alcohol to school. I'd try and take something that was clear because then it would look like water. So usually it was vodka or white rum. And I'd keep it in a juice bottle in the top of my locker.

I never paid for any of my own alcohol. I would steal it from my parents' liquor cabinet or I'd steal it from my friends or my friends would get it for me. There were always ways to get alcohol without paying for it, so money wasn't really a problem.

Sometimes I would go over to a friend's house and if I had my gym bag with me, I'd have a juice bottle or something in it. If they went upstairs or left me alone with their alcohol, I would pour some into my juice bottle and put the bottle back in the cabinet before their parents would see it.

Once my friend was introducing me to a new boyfriend and I pulled alcohol out of his liquor cabinet and I didn't even know the guy. I feel really bad about it now. My friend still doesn't know I did this.

When I was drinking, I became a totally different person. I could be very cunning, very vindictive, very sly, and it was all alcohol. Everything I did, it was the alcohol that was doing it. Just trying to get that drink, it would make me steal. I could never steal anything now. The guilt would kill me. But alcohol changes you—your whole personality. And even though, on the outside, I looked like this really friendly person and I'd be so outgoing,

I could turn around and steal from you. I scared myself sometimes with these personality changes. Your moods just swing.

Sometimes I had blackouts. I'd do things and I'd wake up the next morning and my friends would tell me, "Well, you did such and such," and I'd say, "Oh, did I?" And I wouldn't—I still can't remember the things I did.

One time my mother was away for the week and my friend had come over to stay at my place. One night she decided she was going to get her hair cut at the hairdresser's so I went with her. And I was very drunk. She was sitting in the chair getting her hair cut—I don't remember any of this, this is just what my friend told me—and I jumped in the chair and said, "That looks like fun—cut my hair too." And the next morning I woke up not remembering anything. I kind of walked by the mirror and went, "Oh!" All my hair was gone.

I started yelling at my friend, "You cut my hair! You cut my hair while I was asleep."

"No I didn't. You went and got it done yourself." To this day I still don't remember getting it done. As hard as I try, I can't remember. I just remember getting up the next morning and taking a fit at my friend.

Wanting to change but . . .
After a while, the personality swings scared me. It really started to scare me when I could be so nice to someone, then turn around and steal from them or talk about them behind their back. And I realized that I was not like that, that before I started drinking, I couldn't do that.

It was the alcohol doing that to me, and I wanted to stop. But I couldn't do it on my own. I needed help and I didn't know how else to get help. All I knew was to drink. So I would drink and basically that was me yelling, "I need help. Somebody help me change myself. I can't do it by myself."

I didn't go to my mom or dad because I didn't think they would listen. I hated myself so much that I didn't think anything I had to say was worth listening to, even if it meant that I was really messed up. I just couldn't tell them. I didn't think they'd listen or I thought they'd make fun of me or tell me that I was just imagining things.

I felt very isolated. I had a lot of friends, acquaintances around me. Like there was always people around me but I felt extremely alone. I felt like I had dug a hole in the ground and I was down in this hole and I couldn't get out. That's how isolated I felt.

When I was really depressed and lonely, I would often blame my parents. Why can't they see this, why can't they see that I'm this lonely and why don't they help me?

Then I would feel really guilty because I'd think, well they've got their own problems, it's all my fault. I should go to them and say, "Listen, I feel really bad. Somebody help me." But I couldn't do that. When I was so alone I felt, it's my own fault. I should go out and meet people. I should go out and say to somebody, "I'm hurting, help me." But it's not that easy.

Physically the alcohol didn't really affect me. I had the shakes every now and then but that was about all. I didn't get hangovers very much. I think that's a negative point on my part because maybe if I had gotten hangovers, I would have stopped drinking a lot earlier. But I never got hungover. I could wake up and drink again.

I'm a small person and it shocked me that I built up a tolerance that was so high and I wouldn't get hangovers or anything.

In my heaviest drinking period, I'd get up in the morning, have a couple of drinks, go to school. During school hours, I'd have about two drinks. So that would be about five. Then I'd come home and I'd drink a little more, so I'd have about seven drinks a day. Seven drinks was about my highest and four would be my lowest. And that was every day for about four years, off and on.

Getting caught and getting help

One day I got suspended from school. The vice principal decided he was going to do a locker check. I think he was already suspicious that I had been drinking. He found alcohol in my locker, so I was suspended for a day and my parents were called in and they found out about it. When that happened, I decided that I was drinking too much and I got myself into treatment.

I felt a great sense of relief. I think a lot of the reason I was drinking at that point was to get attention. It was a cry for help: "Somebody help me, I'm not feeling good about myself."

At the time I got caught I was really depressed and alcohol was even starting not to make me happy any more. I was thinking suicide. I think if I hadn't gotten caught, I would have killed myself. I was really depressed.

I had tried suicide but I chickened out. People say, "That was really good—you chickened out." But I'm afraid of pain so I'm not really a candidate for suicide.

When I was suspended it was kind of a relief: They're going to call my parents and this is going to be over now. Somebody else can handle it. But what I then realized was nobody else was going to just take the problem away. I had to work for it. But I was scared too. I was scared that my parents were going to be really mad.

They were disappointed in me, I think, more than anything else. They felt that they hadn't done their job or whatever. But they were supportive of me when I went into treatment. They didn't really understand what was the matter with me, but I think more than anything, they were disappointed.

The treatment was really strange. It was something totally new for me. All these people were there and they wanted to help me and it was kind of overwhelming at first. I hated it. I just didn't want to go back and that was it. I wasn't going.

But when I got there, all these people were there and they were all trying to help me and it gave me this really good feeling and I didn't want to leave when it was over.

How do I cope?
Peer pressure to drink is there and it's very strong. If you're a teenager, every teenager has experienced peer pressure to drink or to do drugs. But I think it's up to the individual. I don't think you should drink after what I've been through. I mean if you handle it, that's fine, but if you see yourself getting into trouble, you have to get help. You can't do it on your own.

I've been through counselling and I'm still in counselling. They say that if you have an alcoholic in your family, he's sick, but the family is just as sick as he is because you go through the motions—like, my family's great, nothing's wrong, everything's fine—but really it's not. And people get confused as to why this is going on in their family. I think people need a lot of help and the family needs a lot of help as well, to understand what's going on.

When I went into detox, my finger dexterity was shot because of the alcohol. You had to have a physical examination by a doctor when you first went in. She told me to take off my shirt and it took me a minute and a half to get each button undone. I just thought I was clumsy but she said to me, that's the alcohol that has numbed your fingertips. It was very scary to think that I had drunk so much that I was incapable of undoing my own buttons. I sat there and thought: I'm never going to be able to dress myself again. But it cured itself. I can now undo my buttons by myself.

I sometimes have memory lapses or I can be sitting here talking to you and totally lose my train of thought and have no idea what I was saying. That doesn't happen very often any more, and it seems that the longer that I don't drink, the better that my memory is getting.

So I'm not concerned about my future, about the effects alcohol has had on my body. I think I'm young and I've stopped drinking at a young enough age that these things will take care of themselves as I get older.

Now, there's days where I feel like I could take on the whole world, that everything's great. But I still have my days where I wake up and I just stay in bed, forget school. But I mean everybody has their good days and their bad days. It's just that my good days really feel good now.

Staying clean

It's not easy to stay clean. But I know I have to keep striving for that in order to be myself. I have to stay away from alcohol. It is extremely difficult.

I think it's even more difficult when you're a teenager because all these people are saying, "You're just a teenager. You can't be an alcoholic. Have a drink."

But they don't realize that if I have that one drink I'm going to want another and then I'm going to want another, and then it's going to be to the point where I'm just not going to care. Just give me the whole bloody bottle and I'll guzzle it all down.

But you have to take it one day at a time. You have to wake up in the morning and you have to say to yourself, "Today I am not going to drink." And when you go to bed that night, you thank yourself. You congratulate yourself and say, "That's really good, you made it the whole day without a drink. I might drink tomorrow but today I'm going to stay sober." And then you just keep doing that one day at a time. It's very hard.

I don't know if I'm an alcoholic. Right now, I don't think so but if I had kept going at the point I was going, yes, I would be an alcoholic. I think that the potential is there for me but I don't want to reach that stage. I don't want to get that bad that I have to say that I'm an alcoholic, so I'm just staying away from it completely now.

I do have slips though. I was at a party two weeks ago and a lot of my friends were drinking. I had just finished doing a musical and it was the cast party and all my friends were saying, "You've worked really hard on this play. Just celebrate." And I did. And I mean I feel bad about that but I woke up the next day and I said, "Well, I've got to do it again, one day at a time. Let's start all over again." So I hope now that I'm finished with that. I've been clean for two weeks, but before that, it had been three weeks. I had been at another party and done the same thing. But before that I had been clean for eight months.

My friends support me quite a bit. I don't think they fully understand the extent of my problem. I have another friend who just stopped drinking about four weeks ago and so we're kind of in it together. We're kind of saying to each other, "One day (at a time). We'll make it through today if we're both here for each other." He's my ex-boyfriend too, which kind of makes it interesting but we're very good friends now. And all of my friends are basically very supportive of me.

My relationship with my mom is pretty good. I mean she still does things that really bug me. I think maybe even it might just be that we're so much alike. She thinks our relationship is great. When I moved out of her house, she couldn't understand why. She thought we just had the best relationship.

I don't know if it's just me but I don't feel like I can talk to her about my problems—and maybe that's normal. A lot of teenagers feel they can't talk to their parents, but we get along. When we're together, we get along pretty well.

She doesn't drink in front of me. She says she's been clean for two years and I believe her. But our relationship is much different since I moved out of the house. We're more like friends than parent and child. We get along pretty well.

What do I do instead of drinking?

I have many substitutes for alcohol now that I'm clean. I like to sing and act. It gives me a good feeling when I'm up on the stage and the audience is clapping for me. That gives me the highest high I ever had.

Another substitute for alcohol is horseback riding. I live on a farm and I've been horseback riding for about two years. When I'm riding, I feel very good about myself, better than alcohol ever made me feel. When it's just you and the horse and you're riding through a field, I get this amazing sense of pride in myself. When I'm riding, I know that there's nothing I can't do, that alcohol will never make me feel this good.

Advice to others?

If you're really depressed, don't look to alcohol or drugs for your escape. It might give you an escape for a couple of hours but after that, you're just going to feel the exact same way.

If you're feeling very depressed and very alone, call someone or go to a counsellor, talk to anyone. I know you're thinking: Well, if I call someone I don't really know them and it's hard to talk to somebody over the phone. But these people have been trained and they do care or they wouldn't be there.

If you call someone, they'll be able to give you other numbers in your area you can call. Another good way is if you have been drinking and you're depressed and you think you're going to drink again, call Alcoholics Anonymous in your area. They will connect you right away with someone who has been there. They have a direct telephone line that they can get in contact with another alcoholic who has been there and has recovered and that often is a very big help.

◆

Insights and Outlooks

1. Why did Teresa start drinking? Why do you think she feels the way she does? Have you ever had similar feelings? How have you dealt with them?
2. Teresa says, "Peer pressure to drink is there and it's very strong . . . Every teenager has experienced peer pressure to drink or to do drugs." Do you agree with this statement? How can you deal with peer pressure?
3. What is alcoholism? Find out more about alcoholism and teen drinking in Canada. How many teens below the legal age drink? Where can people go for help? Present your findings to the class.
4. Write a letter to Teresa discussing her problem and expressing your feelings to her.

SHOPLIFTING:
GIRLS WHO STEAL

———◆———

James Thornton

An estimated ten billion dollars worth of
consumer goods are stolen from retail stores each year.
Most law enforcement officers believe that
teenagers account for nearly half of all
shoplifting arrests.

Each week before they go out to steal, Lisa* and her best friend Deirdre meet at the Orange Julius in the mall. The two girls hunkered down like conspirators in the back booth seem like average, middle class fifteen-year-old shoppers. What sets them apart from many of those around them is the subject of their hushed conversation: not school or sports or parental injustice, but security systems, suspicious clerks, escape strategies, and this week's list of targets.

Today, like every time they do this, Lisa feels the butterflies in her stomach give way to increasing rushes of adrenaline—a kind of living fear she finds almost pleasurable, especially when compared to the boredom she says she usually feels. Deirdre announces she'll go for a pair of earrings in the mall's most expensive department store; Lisa decides to boost a wallet or a belt in an adjacent section. The two stand up and walk, as casually as they can, over to the store's entrance, where they quickly split up.

At first, Lisa sneaks several looks of support over at her friend, two aisles away, but soon her mind becomes focused entirely on her own theft. Her heart pounds as she approaches a display rack of wallets. One is made of snakeskin dyed bright pink—it's unlike any wallet she's ever seen, and she knows at that moment she has to have it.

Lisa lingers by the countertop rack. Her back feels tingly, almost hot, as if someone's eyes are bearing down on her. She glances around and sees no one. Then, fearing a salesperson might ask her if she wants help, Lisa makes her move—casually, almost accidentally, slipping the pink wallet

---

* All teenagers' names have been changed.

up her sleeve. If caught, she tells herself, she can feign astonishment—*Oh my God! I didn't realize it! How did that get in there?*

As she lifts the wallet, her heart feels like it's going to explode. Suddenly, she feels a fleeting regret—*Why did I do this! Put it back!*—but she knows she doesn't want to put it back, and she tells herself she's more likely to be caught slipping it out of her sleeve than slipping out of the store entirely.

For the next three minutes, Lisa pretends to do some more casual shopping, all the while watching for clerks who might be following her. Deirdre, she notices, has already left, and Lisa wonders briefly what her friend took. Then she heads for the entrance, takes a deep breath, and— though every muscle in her body urges her to run—walks calmly out the door. No one stops her.

"Whadya get? Whadya get?" asks Deirdre at a public telephone, their prearranged meeting spot. Lisa shows off the wallet, and Deirdre pulls out a pair of silver earrings. The conversation, however, quickly turns from the stolen items to the act of stealing. Each boasts about her up-the-sleeve technique, and Deirdre speculates on possible store detectives. After ten minutes, Lisa finally feels her heart rate returning to normal, though she still doesn't feel completely home free. It's at this point that the girls' respective fathers arrive to take them home.

On the ride home, Lisa has little to say to her father, who happens to be a minister. She knows what she has just done is wrong, but it's almost as if somebody else temporarily stepped in and stole this incredible wallet. At her house, she runs to her room and locks the door, for the first time feeling completely safe. She opens a drawer and spreads out jewelry, lipstick, and other previously shoplifted items on her bed. Then, as a kind of centerpiece, she lays down the wallet.

Lisa's pride over this new acquisition is mixed with guilt, and she tells herself this is the last time she will steal. "But the urge for something new always comes back," she says. The following Saturday, Lisa and Deirdre meet again at the back booth.

An estimated ten billion dollars worth of consumer goods are boosted, clipped, kyped, lifted, bagged, thieved, raided, ripped off, or otherwise stolen from retail stores each year. Precise statistics are hard to come by, but most law enforcement experts believe that teenagers account for nearly half of all shoplifting arrests. (Boys, incidentally, are as likely to shoplift as girls.)

And arrest records represent only the iceberg's tip. Lisa and Deirdre admit to stealing "at least a dozen times" without having been arrested, and they believe their technique is improving, making them less likely to be caught in the future. Such thinking has a strong flavor of rationalization and fantasy. For those who persist in stealing, getting caught is often just a matter of time.

"People have tried to come up with the reason why kids steal," says Jeff Gottlieb, PhD, a clinical psychologist who runs a program for shoplifters in Minnesota. "But the only way you can generalize is that shoplifting fulfills some need in a person. This can be financial, or the need for a thrill or approval, or for a host of other reasons."

A small percentage of teenagers shoplift out of a psychological compulsion—like kleptomania. Another small but growing percentage are motivated by a need for money to buy drugs. Most teenagers who steal however, have more ordinary motives. In a survey conducted by the National Crime Prevention Council, the most common reason given by offenders was that they wanted something for free. "You'll find kinds who want, say, a pair of Air Jordans but might not be able to afford them," says Hubert Williams, president of the Police Foundation, in Washington, D.C. Though, of course, plenty of rich kids shoplift, too.

Still tons of kids want things they can't afford and they don't shoplift—because they're afraid, because they worry about getting in trouble, because it's illegal, because it's just not right. They'll try to earn money or might ask their parents for it. Plenty learn to live without things they want. To steal simply isn't seen as a choice.

When shoplifting becomes a real option, there's some skewed rationalization involved. "At first you think a lot about what you're doing and the fact that it's wrong," says Lisa. "But after a while, it becomes less and less real somehow. It becomes such a game you don't worry anymore if it's right or wrong." Other kids justify the crime—saying the store charges too much or what they're taking is insignificant or it won't hurt anybody—and try to convince themselves that it's all right to steal.

Stealing with friends diffuses the responsibility, too. "It gives you courage," admits Lisa, "and it doesn't seem like it's so bad if somebody else is doing it with you."

Regardless of motive, "shrinkage" due to shoplifting and employee theft contributes to the majority of retail business failures. The red ink from shoplifting is also passed on to consumers. (An average family of four would save more than a thousand dollars a year if all shoplifting suddenly stopped.) Ironically, the customers hit hardest are honest teenagers. "Shoplifters make store owners suspicious of *all* teenagers," says Jean O'Neil, a research director at the National Crime Prevention Council. What's more, popular status goods—everything from hot sneakers to sunglasses to electronic games—are the most likely things to be slapped with inflated price tags. So those who don't steal are paying a kind of double tax—in reputation and in dollars—to subsidize those who opt for the five-finger discount.

The nation's retailers have fought back, spending billions on guards and on high-tech security devices: electronic tags, hidden camera systems, even subliminal "be honest" messages. Store owners have learned the hard way that letting a shoplifter off with just a warning only earns the store a reputation for being an easy mark, and losses climb.

When a teenager is caught shoplifting, he or she is likely to be handed over automatically to the police, who will occasionally handcuff the shoplifter before taking him or her down to the station for fingerprinting and processing. A "high profile" arrest like this can be devastating, especially when friends see it happen. When Neil, sixteen, was apprehended wearing an overcoat with secret pockets filled with stolen goods, three police officers surrounded him. "One of them grabbed me and put on handcuffs so tight that my thumb went numb," recalls Neil. "They asked me all these questions right in the middle of the mall. I wanted to die."

It's true that the majority of teenagers who steal stop after a few times. Shoplifting is likely to lose its thrill. The guilt of lying compounds the guilt of stealing, and many teenagers eventually feel the goods are no longer worth the pressure and the stress—or the regret. "The guilt is something you can't take back," says Lisa. "You can't make it go away."

For those who find themselves heavily involved in shoplifting, the prospects are more mixed. "Repeated shoplifting could indicate trouble at home or at school," says Dr. Gottlieb. "It could be depression. In some way the person's needs are not being met." For Lisa and Deirdre and many girls like them, it's possible to stop before they find themselves embroiled in the legal system. But quitting cold turkey and without help, as Lisa has already discovered, can be difficult. "It's hard for us to make a dent in someone who truly doesn't feel any guilt; but we can reach the ones who still feel a little bad about what they're doing," says Dr. Gottlieb. "Shaming people, of course, doesn't make them stop shoplifting. But they need to realize they made a mistake."

"Some people shoplift a lot and don't get caught. Or they do it once and get caught," says Sergeant Gene Adamczyk of the Michigan State Police. "Either way, it lessens your moral values. It costs us all in the long run."

◆

Insights and Outlooks

1. Why, according to this article, do teenagers shoplift? What motivates them? How do you think they can be helped?

2. How do the repeat shoplifters justify or rationalize what they are doing? Do you think there are people who truly don't feel any guilt?

3. Debate whether or not you feel it is fair that the large number of teenage shoplifters make store owners suspicious of *all* teenagers.

4. Rewrite the descriptive passage about Lisa's successful shoplifting experience to show her getting caught.

INSTITUTIONALIZED RACISM AND CANADIAN HISTORY: NOTES OF A BLACK CANADIAN

◆

Adrienne Shadd

"If the only image you have of black women is derived from the one on your pancake box, then there is something wrong with the media portrayal of racial minorities."

It always amazes me when people express surprise that there might be a "race problem" in Canada, or when they attribute the "problem" to a minority of prejudiced individuals. Racism is, and always has been, one of the bedrock institutions of Canadian society, embedded in the very fabric of our thinking, our personality.

I am a fifth-generation black Canadian who was born and raised in a small black farming village called North Buxton, near Chatham, Ontario. North Buxton is a community comprised of the descendants of the famous Elgin Settlement of escaped slaves who travelled the Underground Railroad to freedom in Canada in the 1850s. As a young girl growing up in the fifties and sixties, I became aware of the overt hostility of whites in the area when we would visit nearby towns. Children would sometimes sneer at us and spit, or call us names. When we would go into the local ice cream parlour, the man behind the counter would serve us last, after all the whites had been served, even if they came into the shop after us. Southwestern Ontario may as well have been below the Mason-Dixon line in those days. Dresden, home of the historic Uncle Tom's Cabin, made national headlines in 1954 when blacks tested the local restaurants after the passage of the Fair Accommodation Practices Act and found that two openly refused to serve them. This came as no surprise, given that for years certain eateries, hotels, and recreation clubs were restricted to us, and at one time blacks could only sit in designated sections of movie theatres (usually the balcony), if admitted at all. Yet this particular incident sent shock waves through the nation, embarrassed about such evidence of racial "intolerance" going on in its own backyard.

Somehow, this kind of racism never bothered me. I always felt superior to people who were so blind that they could not see our basic humanity. Such overt prejudice, to my mind, revealed a fundamental weakness or fear. Although, instinctively, I knew that I was not inferior, there was not one positive role model outside our tiny community, and the image of blacks in the media was universally derogatory. Africans were portrayed as backward heathens in the Tarzan movies we saw, and black Americans were depicted through the characters of Step 'n Fetchit, Amos 'n Andy, Buckwheat of "Our Gang" fame, or the many maids who graced the television and movie screens in small bit parts. (Black Canadians were virtually nonexistent in Canadian media.) I used to wonder if it could really be true that black people the world over were so poor, downtrodden, inarticulate, and intellectually inferior, as the depictions seemed to suggest.

At the age of 10, we moved to Toronto. In the largely white neighbourhood where we lived, I was initially greeted by silent, nervous stares on the part of some children, who appeared afraid of me, or at least afraid to confront me openly. Later, as I began to develop an awareness of the Civil Rights and Black Power movements through my readings, certain friends would respond with a frozen silence if I brought up the name of Malcolm X, or, for that matter, the latest soul record on the charts. Looking back, I can see that things ran fairly smoothly as long as the question of race could be ignored, and as long as I did not transgress the bounds of artificial "colour blindness" under which I was constrained. This, apparently, was the Torontonian approach to race relations.

I share these reminiscences to illustrate the different forms which racism has taken over time, and in varying locales in Canada, whether in the form of overt hostility and social ostracism as in southwestern Ontario, or in the subtle, polite hypocrisy of race relations in Toronto in the sixties.

But how, you may ask, do these personal experiences represent examples of institutionalized racism? Do they not depend on the attitudes of people, which vary from individual to individual? Are not our Canadian laws and policies very clear about the fundamental rights of all people to equal treatment and opportunities?

The problem with this line of thinking is that it fails to recognize how powerfully attitudes and behaviours are shaped by the social climate and practices around us. If the only image you have of black women is derived from the one on your pancake box, then there is something wrong with the media portrayal of racial minorities. If there are no visible minorities in the boardrooms of the corporate world, and few in positions of influence and authority in the workforce, this sends a message far more potent than the human rights legislation set up to create a more equitable distribution of rewards and opportunities. When generation after generation of school children continue to be taught only about the accomplishments of white Europeans in Canada—mostly men—the myth that this is "traditionally a white country," as I heard a reporter say the other day, will persist, unchallenged.

The selective recording of some historical events and the deliberate omission of others have not been accidental, and they have had far-reaching consequences. Blacks and other people "of colour" are viewed as recent newcomers, or worse, "foreigners" who have no claim to a Canadian heritage except through the "generosity" of Canadian immigration officials, who "allow" a certain quota of us to enter each year.

But this myth that Canada is a white country is insidious because, on the one hand, it is so ingrained in the national consciousness, and on the other hand, so lacking in foundation. There is a tendency to forget that Native peoples were here first; blacks, first brought as slaves in the 1600 and 1700s, were among the earliest to settle on Canadian soil; the presence of the Chinese is traced to the 19th century. In fact, people from a wide variety of races and nationalities helped to build this country. Unfortunately, this really is not reflected in our school curricula.

The long black presence and contribution to Canada's development continues to go unacknowledged. People are surprised to learn, for example, that 10% of the Loyalists who migrated to British North America after the American Revolution were black. Their descendants, particularly in the Maritimes, have been living in quasi-segregated communities for over 20 years. Blacks were one of the largest groups to enter the country during the 19th century when 40-60 000 fugitive slaves and free people "of colour" sought refuge in Canada West (Ontario) between 1815-1860.

Standard textbooks never mention that, in 1734, part of the city of Montreal was burned down by Marie-Joseph Angelique, a black female slave, when she learned of her impending sale by her slave mistress. Most Canadians are not even aware that slavery existed in this country. Women's history courses fail to acknowledge that the first newspaper-woman in Canada was a black, Mary Ann Shadd, who edited a paper for fugitives between 1853-1859 in Toronto and later Chatham, Ontario. Heartwarming stories such as that of Joe Fortes—a Barbadian-born sailor who came to British Columbia in 1885 and subsequently, as the lifeguard of English Bay, taught three generations of young people to swim—are all but forgotten. Fortes is considered a true Canadian hero to those who are still around to remember him, but it seems that many younger British Columbians believe Fortes was a white man. And did any of you know that the term "the real McCoy" was coined after the inventions of a black man, Elijah McCoy, born in Harrow, Ontario, in 1840?

Today's students, black and white, look to the United States for information regarding the Civil Rights Movement, unaware that a gripping saga exists right here in Ontario. In the forties and fifties, organizations such as the Windsor Council on Group Relations, the National Unity Association of Chatham-Dresden-North Buxton, the Brotherhood of Sleeping Car Porters, and the Negro Citizens' Association of Toronto fought segregation in housing, accommodations, and employment, as well as racist immigration laws. Much of the antidiscrimination and human rights legislation that we now take for granted are a direct result of the struggles which these groups waged.

* * *

On a more personal level, even the most subtle and polite forms of racism can be detrimental, especially as they affect children. In my own case, when we moved to Toronto I was made to feel different, alien, even though no one specifically referred to my racial origin. It is a feeling which has never fully left me and perhaps explains why to this day I do not feel comfortable in the company of a group of white people. And when some whites think they are paying black people a compliment by saying, "We don't think of you as black," as my sister's friends have told her, this is not just a misplaced nicety; it is an insult. We are not seeking "honorary" white status.

Before we as a society can liberate ourselves from the grip of racism, we have to acknowledge that it exists, and that it is not something which has been blown out of proportion; neither is it the figment of some people's imaginations. If we can do this much, we will at least have moved out from under the heavy shroud of self-delusion and deceit. That in itself would be a refreshing step forward.

---◆---

Insights and Outlooks

1. Why does Adrienne Shadd feel that racism is a problem not just of a few prejudiced individuals, but one that is embedded in our Canadian society? Do you agree with her?

2. What does Adrienne Shadd mean by an "artificial colour blindness"? How did it affect her as a child? Why might it be just as harmful as open prejudice, do you think?

3. List examples of how racial minorities are portrayed in the media today. Do you think the images have changed from the ones mentioned in the essay? If so, how? Do you think the images are realistic?

4. Write an editorial for your student newspaper expressing your point of view on racism in Canada. You could use some of the evidence presented in Shadd's essay as well as your own experience to support your point of view.

A BAG OF POSSIBLES AND
OTHER MATTERS OF THE MIND

———◆———

Robert Fulghum

**"What went wrong between kindergarten and college?
What happened to Yes! of course I can?"**

Since my apotheosis as Captain Kindergarten, I have been a frequent guest in schools, most often invited by kindergartens and colleges. The environments differ only in scale. In the beginners classroom and on the university campuses the same opportunities and facilities exist. Tools for reading and writing and scientific experimentation are there—books and paper, labs and workboxes—and those things necessary for the arts— paint, music, costumes, room to dance—likewise available. In kindergarten, however, the resources are in one room, with access for all. In college, the resources are in separate buildings, with limited availability. But the most radical difference is the self-image of the students.

Ask kindergartners how many can draw—and all hands shoot up. Yes, of course we draw—all of us. What can you draw? Anything! How about a dog eating a firestick in a jungle? Sure! How big you want it?

How many of you can sing? All hands. Of course we sing! What can you sing? Anything. What if you don't know the words? No problem, we can make them up. Let's make them up. Let's sing! Now? Why not!

How many of you dance? Unanimous again. What kind of music do you like to dance to? Any kind! Let's dance! Now? Sure, why not?

Do you like to act in plays? Yes! Do you play musical instruments? Yes! Do you write poetry? Yes! Can you read and write and count? Soon! We're learning that stuff now.

Their answer is Yes! Again and again and again. Yes! The children are large, infinite and eager. Everything is possible.

Try those same questions on a college audience. Only a few of the students will raise their hands when asked if they draw or dance or sing or paint or act or play an instrument. Not infrequently, those who do raise their hands will want to qualify their responses—I only play piano, I only draw horses, I only dance to rock and roll, I only sing in the shower.

College students will tell you they do not have talent, are not majoring in art or have not done any of these things since about third grade. Or worse, that they are embarrassed for others to see them sing or dance or act.

What went wrong between kindergarten and college? What happened to Yes! of course I can?

As I write I am still feeling exuberant from an encounter with the cast of Richard Wagner's opera "Die Walkure." Last night I watched a stirring performance of this classic drama. This morning I sat onstage with the cast and discussed just how the production happens. I especially wanted to know how they went about learning their parts—what strategies they used to commit all to memory.

The members of the cast are students in kindergarten and first grade. They did indeed perform "Die Walkure"—words, music, dance, costumes, scenery, the works. Next year they will do "Siegfried"—already in production—as part of a run through the entire "Ring" cycle. And no, this is not a special school of the performing arts for gifted children. It's the Spruce Street School in Seattle, Wash.

They are performing Wagner because they are not yet old enough to know they cannot. And they understand the opera because they make up stories and songs just like it out of their own lives.

To answer the question, "How do children learn?," I did something schools never do: I asked children. Because they know. They have not been hanging in a closet somewhere for six years waiting for school to begin so they could learn. Half their mental capacity has developed before they come to the schoolhouse door. I repeat for emphasis—they know how to learn.

Brunnhilde, still wearing her helmet, explains that it works best for her if she learns her lines in small sections and then pays careful attention to the first three words of a section and then learns those. In case she needs prompting, just a word or two will set off a chain reaction in her mind. She also switches around and sings the talking words and talks the singing words, doing all of this while she moves around instead of sitting still. Siegfried and Wotan have other methods of their own. All seem to know. All have different ways.

The skeptical author is thinking maybe the children are just doing a trained-seal act—I mean Wagner is heavy stuff—surely they don't really get it. So I ask the young actress playing Brunnhilde to tell me how her character fits into the story. "Do you know about Little Red Riding Hood?" she asks. Yes. "Well it's kind of like that—there's trouble out there in the world for the girl and her grandmother and the wolf and everybody." And then, so I will understand better, she compared the role to that of Lady Macbeth. Yes. She knows about that, too. The school did "Macbeth" last fall. She also talks about "The Hobbit" and "Star Wars" and a radio play the class is writing that is a spoof on all this—"MacDude." "Do you understand?" she asks with concern. I do. And so does she.

(By the way, the only significant deviation from the script came at the very end of "Die Walkure," where Wotan is supposed to take his sleeping daughter in his arms and kiss her eyelids. No way. Art may have its standards, but no 7-year-old boy is going to kiss a girl on her eyelids or anywhere else. There are limits.)

We are sent to school to be civilized and socialized. Why? Because we believe that knowledge is better than ignorance and that what is good for the group and what is good for the individual are intertwined.

As a nation we have concluded that it is better for us all if all of us go to school.

Thomas Jefferson first proposed, in 1779 to the Virginia Legislature, that all children be educated at public expense, but it was not until well into the next century that such a plan was put into place, and even then without enthusiasm on the part of the public. The idea was resisted by a substantial part of the population—sometimes with armed force. As late as the 1880s the law had to be enforced in some towns by militia who marched children to school under guard.

In an aspiring nation in the age of the Industrial Revolution, it became a matter of political economy to have educated citizens.

We still believe that it is important to be sent out of the home into the world to be initiated into society. We call that ritual ground "School." And when we get there we are required to learn the rules and regulations of community, to acquire certain skills and to learn something of human values and the long history of the reaching for light and dignity.

Society puts its best foot forward in kindergarten and first grade.

Want to have an exciting conversation about education? Don't ask someone what they think of the schools. Never. Ask instead that they tell you about the best teacher they ever had. Ask instead that they tell you about the best learning experience they ever had. Ask them if they wish they could sing and dance and draw. Or ask what they are learning now or would like to learn soon. And ask them how they go about learning something. And then ask them if they were to design an educational system to support what they've just said, what would it be like.

There is no such thing as "the" human brain—no generic brain. What we know, how we know it, our strategies for learning and our idiosyncratic ways of being alive, differ significantly from person to person. The implications of this for education are almost overwhelming.

There are as many ways to learn something as there are learners.

There is no one way to be human.

We achieve community with metaphors and consensus.

And this makes a teacher's task impossible.

Unless the teacher sees the task not as one of conveying prescribed information, but a way of empowering the student to continue doing what he came in the door doing pretty well—learning for himself. To do any less is to diminish his self-esteem.

As a teacher of drawing and painting and philosophy in a senior high school for 20 years, I offered a course the students called "drawing for turkeys." The prerequisites for the course, as described in the school catalog: "To qualify, you must think you have no talent or skill in drawing and wish otherwise, hoping that the art fairy will look you up someday. Further, you must be able to tie your shoelaces, write your name and be able to find your way to the studio regularly." The classes were always oversubscribed.

Every student learned to draw competently.

Because drawing is a matter of skill. Skills can be acquired with practice.

Because drawing is a matter of looking closely at something—carefully enough to translate what is seen three dimensionally into the language of two-dimensional line and shape and shadow.

To draw is to look. To look is to see. To see is to have vision. To have vision is to understand. To understand is to know. To know is to become. To become is to live.

And to the student who would acknowledge that she had acquired skills but still could not draw because she had no imagination, I would only say: "Tell me about your dreams at night." And she would—at length. And then I would ask, "Who is doing that inside your head?"

Now if drawing requires careful observation, the acquisition of skill, the application of visionary creative imagination—and that's exactly what graduate school, business, industry, government and these times need— then there is some reason to believe that the arts . . . etc. You take it from there.

After sharing this thinking with parents, they would say they wished they could do what their kids were doing in the drawing class (because they still half believe that all I had done was uncover their particular child's hidden talents). So I would say come on to class. And we had night school for parents. And all the parents (except one) learned to draw competently, taking their drawings home to put in that place of artistic honor—the refrigerator door. (As for the one failure, she taught me humility and pushed my teaching skills and her learning skills as far as possible in the process. She's a good photographer now, though. She sees very well.)

On the occasion of his graduation from engineering college this June (*cum laude*, thank you very much), I gave my number-two son a gift of a "possible bag."

The frontiersmen who first entered the American West were a long way from the resources of civilization for long periods of time. No matter what gear and supplies they started out with, they knew that sooner or later these would run out and they would have to rely on essentials. These essentials they called their "possibles"—with these items they could survive, even prevail, against all odds. In small leather bags strung around their necks they carried a brass case containing flint and steel and tinder to make fire. A knife on their belt, powder and shot and a gun completed the possibles.

But many survived when all these items were lost or stolen.

Because their real possibles were contained in a skin bag carried just behind their eyeballs. The lore of the wilderness won by experience, imagination, courage, dreams, self-confidence—these were what really armed them when all else failed.

I gave my son a replica of the frontiersmen's possibles bag to remind him of this spirit.

In a sheepskin sack I placed flint and steel and tinder that he might make his own fire when necessary; a Swiss Army knife—the biggest one with the most tools; a small lacquer box that contained a wishbone from a Thanksgiving turkey—my luck; a small, velvet pouch containing a tiny bronze statue of Buddha; a Cuban cigar in an aluminum tube; and a miniature bottle of Wild Turkey whisky in case he wants to bite a snake or vise versa. His engineering degree simply attests that he has come home from an adventure in the wilderness.

The possibles bag inside his head is what took him there, brought him back and sends him forth again and again and again.

I kept a journal during the years I taught. And in time I boiled my experience down into some one-line statements that became a personal litany to be said when school began and when school was not going well. You will have found some of these notions already expressed at length in the sections above; for emphasis, I restate them here.

Learning is taking place at all times in all circumstances for every person.

There are as many ways to learn something as there are people.

There is no one way to learn anything—learn how you learn—help the student do likewise.

There is nothing everyone must know.

All I have to do is accept the consequences of what I do not know.

There is no one way to be human.

Imagination is more important than information.

The quality of education depends more on what's going on at home than in the school. And more on what is going on in the student than what is going on in the teacher.

In learning, don't ask for food; ask for farming lessons. In teaching, vice versa.

If nobody learns as much as the teacher, then turn students into teachers.

Every student has something important to teach the teacher.

Discontent and ferment are signs the fires of education are burning well.

In education, look for trouble. If you can't find any, make some.

◆
Insights and Outlooks

1. Are there things you did happily and easily in kindergarten that you would tell someone you can't do today? What are they? Why do you think you would say you can't do them?

2. Think about something you learned today. Then think about how you learned it. What special strategies do you use to learn something? Compare your strategies with those of others in your class.

3. Robert Fulghum suggests that the real "bag of possibles" is inside our heads. What values and attitudes do you think make up the bag of possibles that allows us to learn?

4. Take on Robert Fulghum's challenge. Describe the best teacher or the best learning experience you have ever had. Consider why it was the best.

TIME OFF, TIME OUT

**We have lived not in
proportion to the number of years
spent on the earth, but in
proportion that we have enjoyed.**
Henry David Thoreau

How do you like to spend your leisure time? Maybe you like to live vicariously through the daring exploits of superheroes. Do you dream of your great moment in sports, on the stage, or on the television screen? Are you always ready to rock with your group of choice on the music video channel? Our demand for leisure entertainment has created a fascinating array of pursuits and personalities. One thing they all have in common is that countless people work long and hard to provide us with moments of joy and relaxation.

GREAT KRYPTON! SUPERMAN WAS THE STAR'S ACE REPORTER

Henry Mietkiewicz

**"It came from him being that quiet,
pensive kid who sat there drawing,
and underneath it all really just wanting to
have that strength and that power."**

By the time he was hawking The Daily Star in downtown Toronto in the Roaring Twenties, 9-year-old Joe Shuster had already come to believe he was selling more than mere newspapers.

To this ambitious newsboy, The Star was a passport to wonder.

Within its pages, Joe had discovered the fantasy world of the color comics and, along with it, the inspiration that would make him the co-creator of one of the most illustrious fictional characters of the 20th century: Superman.

Even working as a Star newsboy had long-range effects. By peddling papers amid such imposing office towers as the old Star building on King St. W., Joe was exposed to sights and sounds that would later be incorporated into Superman's home town of Metropolis.

When Superman debuted as the comics sensation of 1938, the Toronto-born cartoonist (who moved to Cleveland at the age of 10) wanted to express his appreciation for those formative, first impressions.

So Shuster gave the name "The Daily Star" to the Metropolis newspaper that employed Superman's alter-ego, mild-mannered reporter Clark Kent.

Not until 1940, on orders from a New York editor, did Shuster—and his partner, writer Jerry Siegel—name the paper the Daily Planet.

Today Shuster smiles as he recalls the excitement of those early days, when Superman's exploits set the standard for a whole new generation of gaudily costumed crime-fighters.

Memories are all that remain for the frail, 77-year-old artist, who neatly tucks his most cherished moments into the dozens of scrapbooks and photo albums that line his simple, one-bedroom apartment in suburban West Los Angeles.*

Mention of The Star sends Shuster scurrying to the cardboard boxes that hold mementoes and treasures from every era—sheet music from the *Superman* Broadway play of 1966, enlarged photocopies of the first Superman sketches from the '30s, a mid-'40s photograph of Siegel, and issues of *Reader's Digest*, *Newsweek* and *Us* that cover-featured the Man of Steel when the *Superman* movie was released in 1978.

Finally, Shuster locates a hardcover book of reprinted Superman stories that were first published in the late '30s. Settling gently on to the sofa, he lowers his head to the glossy pages and squints while looking for a particular comic panel.

The search goes slowly. Blindness and other ailments are slowly overtaking Shuster, who has lost most of the vision in his right eye and uses oversized magnifying glasses to read the mail and make sense of the fleeting images on his television screen.

Even signing his name is a chore. His left hand—the one that once drew colorful figures soaring over futuristic cities—can no longer hold a pencil firmly, while his right hand trembles as he labors to shape the letters.

Siegel, too, is feeling the weight of years and cannot participate in the interview, because he's recovering from heart-bypass surgery.

"There it is," Shuster says, pointing to a picture of Superman descending

---

* Joe Shuster died in the fall of 1992.

toward a Metropolis skyline. The caption on the comic panel says the Man of Steel has landed near the Daily Star building.

"Sure! The Star!" Shuster exclaims, wheezing slightly. "Not The Planet. That came later."

"I still remember drawing one of the earliest panels that showed the newspaper building. We needed a name, and I spontaneously remembered the Toronto Star. So that's the way I lettered it. I decided to do it that way on the spur of the moment, because The Star was such a great influence on my life."

The influence was acquired, quite literally, on his father's knee. Shuster remembers his father, Julius, returning home every evening from his tailor shop in Toronto's garment district, and hoisting his son on to his knee to read him the comics.

Young Joe was enchanted. And on weekends, when the comics were printed in glorious color, they were the ultimate entertainment.

"In those days, color comics were published on a large scale. They would devote an entire page to one comic, usually with vivid colors— very bright, vivid colors.

"Of course, I was only 3 or 4 and I couldn't read. So we had a ritual. We would both open up the color comics and my father would read all the dialogue and balloons. I remember the Katzenjammer Kids, Boob McNutt, Happy Hooligan and Barney Google.

"But my sharpest memory is of Little Nemo. It was a very imaginative strip and it even had a touch of science fiction in it. It had marvellous scenes—Winsor McCay's depiction of the city of the future, the planets— all the things I loved. That was among the things that turned me on to fantasy and science fiction.

"Later on, I began to read the comics myself and I had hopes of someday drawing a comic strip of my own."

It wasn't long before Joe's talent for drawing became apparent. His younger sister, Jean Peavy of Albuquerque, New Mexico, even remembers her 4-year-old brother drawing elaborate scenes on the walls of their Toronto home.

The problem, Peavy says, was that paper was a luxury in a household where money was always tight. Julius, an immigrant from Rotterdam, and Ida, who had come from Kiev, were barely able to make ends meet.

"There were times," Peavy says, "when my mother was able to get Joe some pieces of white paper from the butcher. But that didn't happen often."

Instead, Joe became a scrounger, honing his artistic skill on whatever scraps of discarded paper and bits of cardboard he could find.

"I would go from store to store in Toronto and pick up whatever they threw out," Shuster recalls. "One day, I was lucky enough to find a bunch of wallpaper rolls that were unused and left over from some job.

"The backs were blank, naturally. So it was a goldmine for me, and I went home with every roll I could carry. I kept using that wallpaper for a long time.

"Years later (in the mid-'30s), Jerry and I sold our first two stories to DC Comics—one was about (swashbuckler) Henry Duval and the other was (magician) Dr. Occult. One was drawn on brown wrapping paper and the other was drawn on the back of wallpaper from Toronto.

"And DC approved them, just like that! It's incredible! But DC did say, 'We like your ideas, we like your scripts and we like your drawings. But please, copy over the stories in pen and ink on good paper.'

"So I got my mother and father to lend me the money to go out and buy some decent paper—the first drawing paper I ever had—in order to submit these stories properly to DC Comics."

Shuster's recollections of Toronto are happy ones, although he does remember his family having to move regularly, most likely when rent became a problem. Details are hazy now, but he recalls living on Bathurst, Oxford and Borden Sts. and attending Ryerson and Lansdowne Public Schools.

Joe was also greatly impressed by Toronto's vitality and size, especially when he became a newsboy and began to get a clearer sense of his surroundings.

When, in the '30s, it came time for him to draw the skyline and landmarks of Metropolis, Shuster dismissed Cleveland from his mind and turned instead to memories of Toronto.

"Cleveland was not nearly as metropolitan as Toronto was, and it was not as big or as beautiful. Whatever buildings I saw in Toronto remained in my mind and came out in the form of Metropolis.

"As I realized later on, Toronto is a much more beautiful city than Cleveland ever was." Pausing for a moment, Shuster chuckles and adds, "I guess I don't have to worry about saying that now."

Even after Julius moved the family to Cleveland in 1924 for business reasons, Joe maintained his Canadian link through a close friendship with his cousin, Frank—the same Frank Shuster of the Wayne and Shuster comedy team.

Interestingly, Joe and Frank were double first-cousins: Their fathers

(Julius and Jack) were brothers and their mothers (Ida and Bessie) were sisters.

Jean Peavy even recalls that at one point, her family and Frank's family cut expenses by sharing a house—Frank Shuster downstairs and Joe Shuster upstairs.

Joe and Frank became ardent movie-goers, often spending entire days together watching the silent pictures in the downtown theatre where Frank's father (Joe's uncle Jack) worked as a projectionist.

In later years, when Shuster tried to imagine what Superman and his friends would look like, he drew upon actors in the movies he'd seen in Toronto with Frank.

Superman, with his heroic physique and glowing optimism, was patterned largely after Douglas Fairbanks Sr. And Clark Kent—his name derived from movie stars Clark Gable and Kent Taylor—was a combination of timorous, bespectacled Harold Lloyd and pale, mild-mannered Joe Shuster himself.

(Lois Lane, by the way, came not from the movies, but was modelled on Joanne Carter, who later became Jerry Siegel's wife.)

But could that be right—Joe Shuster as Clark Kent? "No question about it," says Frank Shuster, who spent summer vacations with his cousin in Cleveland and watched Joe's talent develop.

"I'd try to get him to come out and play ball," Frank says, "because I was a much more active and physical kind of guy. I'll admit that Joe believed in lifting weights and making himself strong, but he was never one for actual activity.

"He looked like the stereotypical, 90-pound weakling getting sand kicked in his face. And it later occurred to me that he *was* Clark Kent— the sort of nebbish in glasses that everyone wanted to kick around—but underneath he was the Man of Steel.

"It came from him being the quiet, pensive kid who sat there drawing, and underneath it all, really just wanting to have that strength and that power."

Power—and fame—were showered on Shuster and Siegel within months of Superman's first appearance in June, 1938, in *Action Comics* no. 1. Among the first publications to acknowledge the character's impact was *Time* magazine, followed closely by The Toronto Star.

"I do remember that when Superman was sold, The Star was one of the first to send a reporter," Joe Shuster says with a smile. "That's another reason I'm grateful. They called long-distance to set up an interview. And then, I remember being interviewed by The Star in New York, soon after Superman became a success."

Before long, Shuster and Siegel had time for little else but scripting and drawing Superman—one story a month in *Action Comics*, three or four stories in the quarterly (and later bi-monthly) *Superman Comics*, a daily and weekend newspaper strip, and a host of merchandising spinoffs.

The workload kept Shuster tied to his easel, but he did manage one, final visit to Toronto in December, 1941, to be best man at his cousin Frank's wedding.

While in town, he also attended a benefit at the Eaton Auditorium hosted by The Toronto Star Santa Claus Fund. The highlight of the show was an auction of an original painting of Superman by Shuster, with proceeds going to needy children.

Today, despite his illness and the professional setbacks of the '50s and '60s, Shuster still thinks of those less fortunate than himself.

One corner of his apartment is jammed with stereo components— three turntables, several tapedecks and amplifiers, a number of CD players and a dozen high-power speakers—that will be donated to the visually impaired.

Classical music, especially his rare collection of opera overtures, is among his greatest pleasures and he never misses the chance to get the most out of his recordings by acquiring the latest in audio technology— even if it means giving away equipment that's less than a year old.

But, Shuster says, the biggest thrill is knowing that new generations of comics fans are growing up with Superman, even if the Man of Steel is drawn by other hands.

"There aren't many people who can honestly say they'll be leaving behind something as important as Superman. But Jerry and I can, and that's a good feeling. We're very, very proud and happy and pleased."

◆

Insights and Outlooks

1. Why do you think Joe Shuster created Superman? What was his motivation and his inspiration?

2. What qualities do you think have allowed Superman to maintain his superhero status for over 50 years?

3. What is an alter-ego? Why do you think Joe Shuster gave Superman an alter-ego —Clark Kent?

4. In groups, discuss what qualities a superhero (male or female) would need to have audience appeal into the next century? Create a drawing or a comic strip featuring this superhero.

OPEN NET

George Plimpton

**What would it be like to suddenly find yourself
playing goal for an NHL hockey team?**

The account which follows is a description of what it is like for an amateur
to find himself in the exalted world of the professional—in this case playing
in the goal for the Boston Bruins in an exhibition game in Philadelphia's
Spectrum against the Flyers. Ice hockey was one game I never thought I
would attempt as a participatory journalist. I am very poor on skates. I have
weak ankles. Friends joke that I am the same height on the ice as I am off. I
trained with the Bruins for a month. They were in a constant state of
merriment about my troubles on the ice—especially my inability to stop
sharply. Often I would crash into the boards to stop. The Bruins joked that I
was the only hockey player in the National Hockey League who would
check *himself* into the boards. My stay with the Bruins is recounted in a
book entitled *Open Net*, from which this extract is taken. The scene is the
Bruins' locker room just prior to the game with the Flyers.

We had just a few minutes left. Bridgework was removed: when the teeth
came out and were put in the paper cups, the face took on a slightly
different aspect, collapsing slightly, like the first twinge of an umbrella
being closed. Cheevers leaned across from his stool. He looked very
serious. He had one last thing he wanted me to remember. "Stand up!
Stand up!" he said, meaning, of course, to remind me to keep myself aloft
on the ice, that I was useless if I fell down. Under the stress of the moment I
misunderstood him. I thought he was telling me, for some odd reason, to
stand up there in the locker room. I shot up from my bench abruptly,
towering over him on my skates, and looked down at him questioningly.

"Not in here, for God's sake," Cheevers said. "Out on the ice." He shook
his head. "A basket case."

[Don] Cherry read out the lines: Mike Forbes and Al Sims at defense,
and the McNab line, with Dave Forbes and Terry O'Reilly at the wings,
would start. He read out my name as the goaltender somewhat perfunc-

torily, I thought, making nothing of it in any jocular way, as if it were a perfectly natural choice to make, and then he looked over at me and said: "It's time. Lead them out."

I put on my mask and clumped to the locker room door. I had forgotten my stick. Someone handed it to me. I was the first Bruin in the tunnel. I could hear the Bruins beginning to yell behind me as we started out.

The tunnel to the rink is dark, with the ice right there at its lip, so that one flies out of it, like a bat emerging from a cast-iron pipe, into the brightest sort of light—the ice a giant opaque glass. The great banks of spectators rose up from it in a bordering mass out of which cascaded a thunderous assault of boos and catcalls. Cherry was right. The Bruins were not at all popular in Philadelphia.

We wheeled around in our half of the ice . . . the Flyers in theirs. There was no communication between the two teams; indeed, the players seemed to put their heads down as they approached the center line, sailing by within feet of each other without so much as a glance. Seaweed [Pettie, my training-camp roommate] had told me: "In hockey you don't talk to the guys from the other team at all, ever. You don't pick him up when he falls down, like in football." He told me about a pre-game warm-up in the Soviet-Canada series in which Wayne Cashman had spotted a Russian player coming across the center line to chase down a puck that had escaped their zone; Cashman had skated over to intercept him and checked him violently into the boards. "Well, the guy was in the wrong place," Seaweed said when I expressed my astonishment. "He should have known better."

I skated over to the boards, working at the clasp at my chin to adjust my mask. The fans leaned forward and peered in at me through the bars of the mask—as if looking into a menagerie cage at some strange inmate within. "Hey, lemme see." A face came into view, just inches away, the mouth ajar, and then it withdrew to be replaced by another, craning to see. I could hear the voice on the public address system announcing me as the goaltender for a special five-minute game. The Bruins were motioning me to get in the goal. We were a minute or so away. I pushed off the boards and reached the goal in a slow glide, stopping and turning myself around slowly and carefully.

The three officials came out onto the ice. The organist was playing a bouncy waltzlike tune that one's feet tapped to almost automatically, but I noticed the officials pointedly tried not to skate to its rhythm as they whirled around the rink to warm up, perhaps because they would seem to demean their standings as keepers of order and decorum if they got into the swing of the music. They too came up and inspected me briefly, glancing through the bars of my mask without a word and with the same look of vague wonder that I had noticed from the fans.

The Bruins began skating by, cuffing at my pads with their sticks as they passed. Tapping the goaltender's pads is perhaps the most universal procedure just before the game—in most cases, of course, a simple gesture of encouragement, like a pat on the back, but in other instances a most distinctive act of superstition. The Buffalo Sabres had a player, Ric Seiling, their rightwing, who had it fixed in his head that things would go badly if he were not the last of the starters on the ice to tap the goaltender's pads. The trouble was that the Sabres had another player, a big defenseman, Jerry Korab, of exactly the same inclination. On one odd occasion Bill Inglis, the Sabres' coach, put both men on the ice to start the game; the two of them, as the other players got set, began wheeling around the net, tapping the goaltender's pads, one after the other, to be sure to be the last before the puck was dropped—a sight so worrisome that Inglis made a quick substitution and got one of them out of there.

For me, even as I wobbled slightly in the crease from the impact of some of the stronger blows from my Bruin teammates as they skated by, I felt a surge of appreciation and warmth toward them for doing it. Two of the Bruins stopped and helped me rough up the ice in front of the cage—this a procedure so the goalie gets a decent purchase with his skate blades. Invariably, it is done by the goalie himself—long, scraping side thrusts with skates to remove the sheen from the new ice. It occurred to me later that to be helped with this ritual was comparable to a pair of baseball players coming out to help a teammate get set in the batter's box, kneeling down and scuffing out toe-holds for him, smoothing out the dirt, dusting his bat handle, and generally preparing things for him, as if the batter were as unable to shift for himself as a store-front mannequin. However odd this may have appeared from the stands—the three of us toiling away in front of the net—it added to my sense of common endeavor. "Thank you, thank you," I murmured.

Other Bruins stopped by while this was going on, and peering into my mask they offered last-minute advice. "Chop 'em down! Chop 'em down!" I looked out at Bobby Schmautz and nodded. His jaw was moving furiously on some substance. "Chop 'em down!" he repeated as he skated off. Slowly the other Bruins withdrew, skating up the ice toward the bench or their positions to stand for the national anthem.

I spent the anthem (which was a Kate Smith recording rather than the real article) wondering vaguely whether my face mask constituted a hat, and if I should remove it. My worry was that if I tampered with any of the equipment I might not have it in proper working order at the opening face-off. The puck would be dropped . . . and the Flyers would sail down the ice towards a goaltender who would be standing bareheaded, face down, fiddling with the chin strap of his mask, his big mitt tucked under his arm to free his fingers for picking at the clasp, his stick lying across the top of the net . . . no, it was not worth contemplating. I sang loudly inside my mask to compensate for any irreverence.

A roar went up at the anthem's conclusion—something grim and antici-patory about that welter of sound, as if, Oh my! we're really going to see something good now, and I saw the players at the center of the rink slide their skates apart, legs spread and stiff, their sticks down, the upper parts of their bodies now horizontal to the ice—a frieze of tension—and I knew the referee in his striped shirt, himself poised at the circle and ready for flight once he had dropped the puck, was about to trigger things off. I remember thinking, "Please, Lord, don't let them score more than five"— feeling that a goal a minute was a dismaying enough fate to plead against to a Higher Authority—and then I heard the sharp cracking of sticks against the puck.

For the first two minutes the Bruins kept the play in the Flyers end. Perhaps they realized that a torrid offense was the only hope of staving off an awkward-sounding score. They played as if the net behind them were empty . . . as if their goalie had been pulled in the last minute of a game they had hoped to tie with the use of an extra forward. I saw the leg-pad of the Flyer's goaltender fly up to deflect a shot.

Well, this isn't bad at all, I thought.

There can be nothing easier in sport than being a hockey goalie when the puck is at the opposite end. Nonchalance is the proper attitude. One can do a little housekeeping, sliding the ice shavings off to one side with the big stick. Humming a short tune is possible. Tretiak, the Russian goaltender, had a number of relaxing exercises he would put himself through when the puck was at the opposite end of the rink. He would hunch his shoulder muscles, relaxing them, and he'd make a conscious effort to get the wrinkles out of his brow. "To relax, pay attention to your face. Make it smooth," he would add, the sort of advice a fashion model might tend to.

It is a time for reflection and observation. During a static spell, Ken Dryden from the Montreal goal noticed that the great game clock that hung above the Boston Garden was slightly askew.

With the puck at the other end, it was not unlike (it occurred to me) standing at the edge of a mill pond, looking out across a quiet expanse at some vague activity at the opposite end almost too far to be discernible— could they be bass fishing out there?—but then suddenly the distant, aimless, waterbug scurrying becomes an oncoming surge of movement as everything—players, sticks, the puck—starts coming on a direct line, almost as if a *tsunami*, that awesome tidal wave of the South Pacific, had suddenly materialized at the far end of the mill pond and was beginning to sweep down toward one.

"A tsunami?" a friend of mine had asked.

"Well, it *is* like that," I said. "A great encroaching wave full of things being borne along toward you full tilt—hockey sticks, helmets, faces with no teeth in them, those black, barrel-like hockey pants, the skates, and somewhere in there that awful puck. And then, of course, the noise."

"The noise?"

"Well, the crowd roars as the wings come down the ice, and so the noise seems as if it were being generated by the wave itself. And then there's the racket of the skates against the ice, and the thump of bodies against the boards, and the crack of the puck against the sticks. And then you're inclined to do a little yelling yourself inside your face mask—the kind of sounds cartoon characters make when they're agonized."

"Arrrgh?"

"Exactly. The fact is it's very noisy all of a sudden, and not only that, but it's very crowded. You're joined by an awful lot of people," I said, "and very quickly. There's so much movement and scuffling at the top of the crease that you feel almost smothered."

What one was trained to do in this situation (I told my friend) was to keep one's eye on the puck at all costs. I only had fleeting glimpses of it—it sailed elusively between the skates and sticks as shifty as a rat in a hedgerow: it seemed impossible to forecast its whereabouts . . . my body jumped and swayed in a series of false starts. Cheevers had explained to me that at such moments he instinctively understood what was going on, acutely aware of the patterns developing, to whose stick the puck had gone, and what the player was likely to do with it. The motion of the puck was as significant to him as the movement of a knight on a chess board. His mind busied itself with possibilities and solutions. For me, it was enough to remember the simplest of Cheever's instructions: "Stand up! Keep your stick on the ice!"

The first shot the Flyers took went in. I had only the briefest peek at the puck . . . speeding in from the point off to my right, a zinger, and catching the net at the far post, tipped in on the fly, as it turned out, by a Philadelphia player named Kindrachuk, who was standing just off the crease. The assists were credited to Rick Lapointe and Barry Dean. I heard this melancholy news over the public address system, just barely distinguishing the names over the uproar of a Philadelphia crowd pleased as punch that a Bruins team had been scored on, however circumspect and porous their goaltender.

Seaweed had given me some additional last minute tips at training camp on what to do if scored upon. His theory was that the goaltender should never suggest by his actions on the ice that he was in any way responsible for what had happened. The goalie should continue staring out at the rink in a poised crouch (even if he was aware that the puck had smacked into the nets behind) as if he had been thoroughly screened and did not know the shot had been taken. In cases where being screened from the shot was obviously not a contributing cause of the score, Seaweed suggested making a violent, abusive gesture at a defenseman, as if that unfortunate had made the responsible error.

When the Flyer goal was scored, I had not the presence or the inclination to do any of the things Seaweed had recommended. I yelled loudly in dismay and beat the side of my face mask with my catching glove. I must have seemed a portrait of guilt and ineptitude. "I didn't see the damn thing!" I called out. As I reached back to remove the puck, the thought pressed in on my mind that the Flyers had scored on their very first attempt—their shooting average was perfect.

What small sense of confidence I might have had was further eroded when soon after the face-off following the Philadelphia goal, one of the Bruins went to the penalty box for tripping; the Flyers were able to employ their power play, and for the remainder of the action, the puck stayed in the Bruins zone.

I have seen a film taken of those minutes—in slow motion so that my delayed reactions to the puck's whereabouts are emphasized. The big catching mitt rises and flaps slowly long after the puck has passed. There seems to be a near-studied attempt to keep my back to the puck. The puck hits my pads and turns me around, so that then my posture is as if I wished to see if anything interesting happened to be going on in the nets behind me. While the players struggle over the puck, enticingly in front of the crease, the camera catches me staring into the depths of the goal, apparently oblivious of the melee immediately behind me.

The film also shows that I spent a great deal of the time flat on the ice, alas, just where Cheevers and Seaweed had warned me not to be. Not much had to happen to put me there—a nudge, the blow of the puck. Once, a hard shot missed the far post, and in reaching for it, down I went, as if blown over by the passage of the puck going by. The film shows me for an instant grasping one of my defensemen's legs, his stick and skates locked in my grasp, as I try to haul myself back upright, using him like a drunk enveloping a lamppost.

Actually, my most spectacular save was made when I was prostrate on the ice . . . the puck appearing under my nose, quite inexplicably, and I was able to clap my glove over it. I could hear the Bruins breathing and chortling as they clustered over me to protect the puck from being probed out by a Flyer stick.

What was astonishing about those hectic moments was that the Flyers did not score. Five of their shots were actually on goal . . . but by chance my body, in its whirlygig fashion, completely independent of what was going on, happened to be in the right place when the puck appeared.

A friend, who was observing from the seats, said the highest moment of comic relief during all this was when one of the Flyers' shots came in over my shoulder and hit the top bar of the cage and ricocheted away.

"What was funny," my friend said, "was that at first there was absolutely no reaction from you at all—there you were in the prescribed position, slightly crouched, facing out towards the action, stick properly down on the ice and all, and then the puck went by you, head-high, and went off that cross-bar like a golf ball cracking off a branch; it wasn't until four or five seconds, it seemed, before your head slowly turned and sneaked a look at where the puck had . . . well . . . *clanged*. It was the ultimate in the slow double-take."

"I don't remember," I said. "I don't recall any clanging."

"Hilarious," my friend said. "Our whole section was in stitches."

Then, just a few seconds before my five-minute stint was up, Mike Milbury, one of the Bruins defensemen out in front of me, threw his stick across the path of a Flyers wing coming down the ice with the puck. I never asked him why. Perhaps I had fallen down and slid off somewhere, leaving the mouth of the net ajar, and he felt some sort of desperate measure was called for. More likely, he had been put up to it by his teammates and Don Cherry. Actually, I was told a *number* of sticks had been thrown. The Bruins wanted to be sure that my experience would include the most nightmarish challenge a goaltender can suffer . . . alone on the ice and defending against a shooter coming down on him one-on-one. The penalty shot!

At first, I did not know what was happening. I heard the whistles going. I got back into the nets. I assumed a face-off was going to be called. But the Bruins started coming by the goal mouth, tapping me on the pads with their hockey sticks as they had at the start of things, faint smiles, and then they headed for the bench, leaving the rink enormous and stretching out bare from where I stood. I noticed a huddle of players over by the Philadelphia bench.

Up in Fitchburg I had been coached on what the goaltender is supposed to do against the penalty shot . . . which is, in fact, how he maneuvers against the breakaway: as the shooter comes across the blue line with the puck, the goaltender must emerge from the goal mouth and skate out toward him—this in order to cut down the angle on the goal behind him. The shooter at this point has two choices: he can shoot, if he thinks he can whip the puck past the oncoming, hustling bulk of the goaltender, slapping it by on either side, or he can keep the puck on his stick and try to come *around* the goalie; in this case, of course, the goalie must brake sharply, and then scuttle backwards swiftly, always maneuvering to keep himself between the shooter and the goal mouth. I would always tell Seaweed or Cheevers, whomever I was chatting with about the penalty shot, that I had to hope the shooter, if this situation ever came up, did not know that I was not able to stop. All the shooter had to do was come to a stop himself, stand aside, and I would go sailing by him, headed for the boards at the opposite end of the rink.

Penalty shots do not come up that often. Gump Worsley in his twenty-one-year career had only faced two, both of which he was unsuccessful against—not surprising perhaps because the goals came off the sticks of Gordie Howe and Boom-Boom Geoffrion. But Seaweed had told me—despite the Gump Worsley statistics—that he thought the chances favored the goaltender . . . that by skating out and controlling the angle the goalie could force the shooter to commit himself. Also, he pointed out that since the shooter was the only other player on the ice, the goaltender always had a beat on the puck, whereas in the flurry of a game he had often lost sight of it in a melee, or had it tipped in by another player, or passed across the ice to a position requiring a quick shift in the goal. Others agreed with him. Emile Francis believed that the goaltender should come up with a save three times out of five. He pointed out while the goaltender is under considerable pressure, so is the other fellow—the humiliation of missing increased because the shooter *seems* to have the advantage . . . the predator, swift and rapacious, swooping in on a comparatively immobile defender. The compiled statistics seem to bear him out. Up until the time I joined the Bruins, only one penalty shot out of the ten taken in Stanley Cup play had resulted in a score—Wayne Connelly's of the Minnesota North Stars in 1968 off Terry Sawchuck.

The confidence that might have been instilled by knowing such statistics was by no means evident in my own case. I stood in the cage, staring out at the empty rink, feeling lonely and put upon, the vast focus of the crowd narrowing on me as it was announced over the public address system that Reggie Leach would take the penalty shot. Leach? Leach? The name meant little to me. I had heard only one thing that I could remember about him from my résumé of Flyers players, which was that he had scored five goals in a play-off game, a record. I dimly recalled that he was an Indian by birth. Also a slap shot specialist . . . just enough information to make me prickle with sweat under my mask.

I gave one final instruction to myself—murmuring audibly inside the cage of my face mask that I was not to remain rooted helplessly in the goal mouth, mesmerized, but to launch myself out toward Leach . . . and just then I spotted him, moving out from the boards, just beyond the blue line, picking up speed, and I saw the puck cradled in the curve of his stick blade.

As he came over the blue line, I pushed off and skated briskly out to meet him, windmilling my arms in my haste, and as we converged I committed myself utterly to the hope that he would shoot rather than try to come around me. I flung myself sideways to the ice (someone said later that it looked like the collapse of an ancient sofa), and sure enough he *did* shoot. Somewhat perfunctorily, he lifted the puck and it hit the edge of one of my skates and skidded away, wide of the goal behind me.

A very decent roar of surprise and pleasure exploded from the stands. By this time, I think, the Philadelphia fans thought of me less as a despised Bruin than a surrogate member of their own kind. The team identification was unimportant. For an instant, I represented a manifestation of their own curiosity if they happened to find themselves down there on the ice. As for the Bruins, they came quickly off the bench, scrambling over the boards to skate out in a wave of black and gold. It occurred to me that they were coming out simply to get me back up on my skates—after all, I was flat out on the ice—but they wore big grins: they pulled me up and began cuffing me around in delight, the big gloves smothering my mask so I could barely see as in a thick joyous clump we moved slowly to the bench. Halfway there, my skates went out from under me—tripped up perhaps or knocked askew by the congratulatory pummels—and once again I found myself down at ice level; they hauled me up like a sack of potatoes and got me to the bench. I sat down. It was a very heady time. I beamed at them. Someone stuck the tube of a plastic bottle in my mouth. The water squirted in and I choked briefly. A towel was spread around my shoulders.

"How many saves?"

"Oh, twenty or thirty. At least."

"What about that penalty shot?"

"Leach is finished. He may not play again. To miss a penalty shot against you? The Flyers may not recover."

I luxuriated in what they were saying.

"Is that right?"

But their attention began to shift back to the ice. The game was starting up again. The sound of the crowd was different: full and violent. I looked up and down the bench for more recognition. I wanted to hear more. I wanted to tell them what it had been like. Their faces were turned away now.

———◆———

Insights and Outlooks

1. Why do you think George Plimpton wanted to play in goal in the NHL? What was he looking for from the experience?

2. Would you say that Plimpton's five minutes in goal was a success or failure? Why? How do you think Plimpton perceives his experience?

3. Plimpton describes several rituals and superstitions associated with the game of hockey. Have you noticed similar rituals in other sports? What is your opinion of this? Is it in good fun, all part of the game, or does it have negative aspects?

4. Create your own participation fantasy. Picture a sport or adventure you may only dream of participating in and then "live" the experience through your writing.

UNFORGETTABLE
JIM HENSON

◆

John Culhane

**"The only way the magic works,"
the Muppets creator said, "is by hard work.
But hard work can be fun."**

Every week across the United States and scores of other countries, millions of children flick on one of the greatest television shows of all time—a show as popular as ever after 21 years.

More incredible still, the cast of characters in this show, imaginatively called "Sesame Street" (after "Open Sesame," the *Arabian Nights* invitation to discovery), is as unlikely a group as the world's children ever took to their hearts. Among the fictional creatures are such funny folk of felt or fur, gazing at you with Ping-Pong-ball eyes, as an uneasy green frog, a royal-blue monster with an insatiable appetite for cookies, and a big, curious, naïve, vulnerable, sympathetic golden bird.

They are the Muppets—one of the most worthwhile creations of popular culture. It is likely that more people can name the Muppet pig (Miss Piggy, femme fatale) who is in love with the Muppet frog (Kermit, "my frog") than can name the capital of Iraq.

Behind this phenomenal show-business success story was Jim Henson, the brilliant creator of the Muppets, who once struggled to explain their phenomenal appeal. "I think it's a sense of innocence, of the naïveté of a young person meeting life. Even the most worldly of our characters is innocent. Our villains are innocent, really. And it's that innocence that is the connection to the audience."

This special distinction, along with an almost childlike genius, echoed through all of Jim's work. "The most sophisticated people I know—inside they're all children," he told me another time. "We never really lose a certain sense we had when we were kids. That sense of looking around at this big world and not knowing who we are and what we're supposed to be doing here." In short, a sense of vulnerability mixed with a larger sense of wonder.

Pretzel Shapes

Starting in 1969, "Sesame Street" brought a rare combination of education and entertainment to its young audience, youngsters roughly two through five years of age—and quicker than you could say "Cookie Monster," these children were learning their letters and numbers and many other things from the Muppets.

When my two sons found out I was going to talk to Jim Henson for an article on "Sesame Street," there was no way they would let me out of our house without tagging along. Indeed, their response to Jim and his Muppets was one of the things that made me realize what a very special person he was.

I remember Jim's warm, gentle-eyed greeting when Michael, T.H. and I showed up on a television sound stage on Manhattan's West Side. Taking us to a table where a Muppet frog lay lifeless, Jim slipped his hand into the piece of fabric and brought him suddenly alive.

"Hey, look!" Kermit told my sons. "I can salute!" And with a deft movement of a rod attached to Kermit's right hand, Jim made the Muppet deliver a snappy salute.

We watched the rehearsal of a scene in which Jim operated a round-faced Muppet named Ernie, and a mustachioed, balding Frank Oz was an oval-headed Muppet named Bert. Standing below an elevated set, both men held their characters over their heads so the camera could see the Muppets, but not Jim and Frank. They kept track of what their Muppets were doing by watching a small monitor below the stage. Often Jim and his fellow Muppeteers had to twist themselves into pretzel shapes to create some of the complicated Muppet routines. Yet what viewers saw on the screen were Muppets moving with astonishing grace.

"Looks like hard work," Michael said when we later watched the same scenes on a TV screen with Jim.

"The only way the magic works is by hard work," he told my sons. "But hard work can be fun." The parent in me cheered.

Watching the TV replay, my younger son, T.H., was amazed. "We didn't see the rods on the screen!" he told Jim.

"They're painted to match the background," the Muppeteer said. "It's important for the illusion that these characters seem to move and think for themselves."

Network Debut

The child in the man was born James Maury Henson in Greenville, Miss., on September 24, 1936. Jim's mother, Elizabeth, was a woman of lively imagination. His father, Paul, was an agronomist with the United States Department of Agriculture, working on pasture crops. (One of these bore the odd name of bird's-foot trefoil, and Jim, forever captivated by funny names, later christened a Muppet after this crop: Herbert Birdsfoot.)

When Paul Henson was transferred to Maryland, the family moved to Hyattsville. In school, Jim was never much of an athlete, but he was always a great dreamer. The last one chosen for baseball games, he would stand dreaming in right field, where there was never much action. That suited him just fine.

In 1949, when he turned 13, the quiet youngster began badgering his parents to buy a new appliance called television, so he could watch the puppet show, "Kukla, Fran and Ollie" and, later, "Life with Snarky Parker." In high school Jim joined a puppet club, and after graduation he landed a job with a local TV station that was looking for young puppeteers.

Continuing to make local TV appearances, Jim enrolled at the University of Maryland, and during his first year was offered a late-night, five-minute TV show in Washington, D.C. He asked Jane Nebel, a fellow art student, to work with him. "It was admiration at first sight," Jane said later.

In 1956, the Muppets made their network television debut on Steve Allen's "Tonight!" show. Jim's Kermit the Frog—fashioned from his mother's old green coat—wore a blond wig and sang "I've Grown Accustomed to Her Face" to an unsightly, purple-faced monster operated by Jane.

"Huge Inspiration"

Jim tried to interest the three U.S. networks in a family variety series built around the Muppets, but was turned down. However, England's Lord Grade liked the idea, and in 1976 put "The Muppet Show" into world distribution from London, combining the biggest American stars—from Bob Hope to Julie Andrews—and the smallest Muppets.

Comedian Mel Brooks, who appeared in *The Muppet Movie*, once said that the basic message of "The Muppet Show" was that "The meek shall inherit the earth."

The Muppets were equally admiring of their guests. Of Ethel Merman, who appeared on the show during its first season, Jim's Kermit once intoned, "When she sings, I get a people in my throat."

Jim and Jane were married in 1959. By the 1970s, Jane was spending most of her time at the Henson home in Bedford, N.Y., raising their five children. An affectionate father, Jim encouraged Brian, Cheryl, Heather, John and Lisa to watch how the Muppet magic was made—and to get involved.

Brian Henson remembers the "huge inspiration" that came from growing up around a man whose special fantasy world was always spilling over into his family. Not surprisingly, all five children have worked in the arts. Brian, like his father, became a puppeteer.

Alter Ego

In all, Jim and his colleagues created more than 2000 rich and woolly and imaginative Muppet characters. Some became superstars—like the seductive Miss Piggy and Cookie Monster (both operated by Frank Oz), Big Bird (Carroll Spinney) and, of course, Jim's own, irrepressible Kermit. "I suppose he's an alter ego," Jim once said, "but he's a little snarkier than I am—slightly wise. Kermit says things I hold myself back from saying."

Yet Kermit, like Jim, was ever the trouper. In a movie back lot in Hollywood, I remember Jim and Kermit aboard a bathysphere, being lowered into a "Georgia swamp" for a scene in *The Muppet Movie*. A log had been fitted on top of the bathysphere, and Kermit was perched on the log. In Jim's tiny submarine compartment was a breadbox-size TV monitor and all six feet, three inches of Jim, jammed into a cross-legged yoga crouch. Air was fed to him through a hose, and electric cables brought him the director's instructions and the picture on the TV monitor.

Through two rubber gloves that came out of the top of the diving bell, Jim manipulated Kermit's mouth with his right hand so Kermit could sing, and with his left hand Jim used a nearly invisible black wire to make Kermit strum the banjo. Jim was underwater for three or four hours at a time.

Why all this? So audiences would better accept the seemingly effortless illusion that Kermit was alive and real.

Galloping Pneumonia

Jim drove himself hard—and the results showed. As of last year "Sesame Street" was being watched by more then 68 percent of all households with a child under age six. "The Muppet Show" plays weekly to 235 million viewers in over 100 countries. Altogether, Jim Henson Productions has won 22 Emmy Awards, with 12 going to Henson personally. His company also won the prestigious Peabody Award in 1978 and again in 1986. Meanwhile, his movies drew millions of fans.

All of this activity, however, wore Jim out. This past May [1990], after appearing on "The Arsenio Hall Show" in Los Angeles, Jim complained of fatigue and a sore throat. Returning to New York with what he thought was the flu, he put off seeing a doctor. When Jane Henson finally got him to New York Hospital, he was having trouble breathing.

An aggressive, overwhelming type of pneumonia known as streptococcus pneumonia Group A had been galloping through his body for at least three days. He was immediately treated with high doses of antibiotics, but the infection had already overwhelmed him. This led to kidney and heart failure, and he died 20 hours later.

At his memorial service, thousands crowded the Cathedral of St. John the Divine in New York. In place of a traditional service, Jim's family substituted a "celebration of life." Mourners waved brightly coloured foam butterflies that were handed out with the memorial programs.

Art of Appreciation

"After the service," says fellow Muppeteer Frank Oz, one of Jim's closest friends, "I wandered around for days and weeks, thinking about Jim. And one image kept coming back to me. It was of Jim standing with his arms folded, wearing a very warm smile, looking, just appreciating.

"Sure, Jim the creator was a genius. Yet I see Jim foremost as an appreciator. He appreciated the Muppet family and his own family. He appreciated flying kites with his children. He appreciated beauty, and he appreciated fun."

And out of that, in turn, Jim made appreciators of the rest of us. We appreciate Jim Henson's brilliance, his joy of life and, especially, the joy he brought to many millions of us around the country—and around the world.

◆

Insights and Outlooks

1. What do you think accounts for the special and vastly popular appeal of the Muppets? Do you agree that they are "one of the most worthwhile creations of popular culture"?

2. If you had to write a character sketch or profile of Jim Henson, what qualities and accomplishments would you stress? How would you describe him to others?

3. What do you think Jim Henson meant when he described Kermit as his alter-ego? If you were to create an alter-ego for yourself, what would it be like?

4. Do you think children see the figures of popular culture as role models? List other modern pop figures (e.g., Barbie, Mickey Mouse), choose three or four of them, and discuss whether you think they are appropriate role models for children. Present your findings to the class.

THE ALANNAH MYLES
STORY

◆

David Henman

**What is the real secret to success
for a Canadian rock star?**

The Ides of March

On Thursday, March 15, [1990] around midday, a chill went up the collective spine of the Canadian music industry as radio announcements, office
chat and telephone conversations revealed the fact that Alannah Myles'
first American single, "Black Velvet," had just bumped Janet Jackson out
of the number one spot on *Billboard* magazine's cherished Top 100. With
lightning speed ("Black Velvet" had been out for less than three months;
furthermore, Janet Jackson was on tour promoting her own record),
Alannah Myles skyrocketed from total obscurity (in the U.S.) to the abso-
lute pinnacle of commercial success—a number one record.

For those embittered souls who are quick to conclude that success like this can only be the result of luck, knowing the right people and a corporate sell-job, stop reading now. Neither this, nor any other similar account is ever going to convince you that success is no accident; or that it is not offered, on a silver platter, to those fortunate few with good looks and a mastery of the science of mediocrity.

The story of Alannah Myles' overnight success (it was a long night—ten years, roughly) is nothing less than an object lesson for every artist in this country who aspires to commercial success, to mainstream recognition of their talents. It is about the three indispensable elements of any kind of success: conviction, or an unwavering belief in yourself; teamwork—a group of people with a shared vision; and perseverance.

Years of Rejection

Recently I came across a demo tape, perhaps the first of many that Alannah had been sending to every record company, big or small, for nearly ten years. What's great about this tape is how awful it is. Unless you believe that the first time Eric Clapton strapped on a guitar and opened his mouth he sounded wonderful, this won't come as a shock. It's the kind of demo that an A&R head would listen to for about thirty seconds and go, "Right. Next?" More to the point, however, it's the kind of forgettable attempt where, after a round of across the board rejections, the artist in question is only too happy to pursue a career in word processing. End of story.

Alannah Myles or, more accurately, the team of Alannah Myles, producer/songwriter David Tyson, manager/songwriter Christopher Ward and entertainment lawyer Stephen Stohn, endured years of rejection. As you'll see as you read on, what initially threatened to destroy their ambition eventually made them that much stronger.

The A&R Department

The first big breakthrough was a three song demo and an accompanying video that landed on the desk of, among others, Rob Roper, former head of A&R for WEA Music Canada and now personal manager for Sharon, Lois and Bram. Like everyone else before, during and since, Roper was impressed with her conviction: "A year and a half ago she was talking about the fifth video for the fifth single. You sort of take that, quite honestly, tongue-in-cheek a lot of the time," chuckles Roper. The timing was off, however. "I had just signed three or four acts, and that put a good-sized dent in my budget. Usually, you sign two or three acts a year, and when you do three or four things in a short space of time, when the fifth one comes along, you've got to take a real hard and fast look at it. Also, at the time, she had no band. She knew who the band was going to be—three out of four members, at least, all top players. There was no management. Christopher was writing songs, he was a (MuchMusic) veejay, he was on the road, etc., etc. So there wasn't what you would call a Bruce Allan in the picture. Given all of that, we decided not to go with it."

However, having just returned from New York on behalf of acts like Blue Rodeo, Roper was privy to the fact that Tunj Arim, Senior V.P. of A&R for Atlantic Records in the U.S., was looking for an "edgy, rock/pop female artist." At Roper's urging, the package was forwarded to Arim.

Much of Alannah's impact on people like Bob Roper stemmed from the fact that her goals were so clearly defined and articulated. "That's part of a selling point," explains Roper, "of any artist who comes through the door. It's the opposite extreme from the artist who calls you up and says, 'I'm a writer; I can do anything you want. What are you looking for? I can do that,' versus somebody coming in who's got a complete package, sitting down and saying, 'This is what I am. This is where I'm going to take it. Do you want to come along for the ride? And, how can you as a label help me attain what it is I want?' It's been her determination that's made this work."

"There was something magic, something different in her voice and her delivery that really touched something in my heart," explains Tunj Arim from his Atlantic Records New York office. "She didn't care if she had to work twenty-four hours a day. That was very rare; usually the artist expects other people to do it for them. She had so many qualities that I really liked the first time I met her."

The lesson here, says Arim, is to never give up. "People don't realize how long it takes. Look at Phil Collins, or Genesis. With Genesis, it took at least eight or nine years."

Tunj Arim is one of the many people aware of Myles' powers of prophecy. "It scares me sometimes. The things that she told me three years ago, about ninety per cent of them have come true."

Management

Danny Goldberg, of Gold Mountain Management, is Alannah's manager for the world and, with Christopher Ward, her co-manager for Canada. Tunj Arim played her demo for Goldberg, to attract his attention. After meeting her he decided he wanted to be involved. "I was real impressed with the music, but I believe that the artist is as important as their music. A lot of very talented people don't have the right attitude. I was very impressed with the clarity of her thought process about what it was that she was doing. She really had a fully developed sense of who she wanted to be as an artist, more so than most new artists. I've really never met anybody that was quite that focused. The other thing that impressed me was that as an artist she marches to the beat of her own drummer. She wasn't just trying to copy what was commercial at the moment. I'm always nervous when artists are overly reactive to what happens to be on the radio at the time. That's kind of like driving by only looking in the rear view mirror. On the artistic side she had almost a rebellious iconoclasm. I've found that the most successful artists are the ones that are a little different from what is going on at the moment rather than the ones who try to synthesize all of the things that are going on."

Myles' attitude towards management, says Goldberg, was very realistic. "She's not into hand-holding. She's always focused on the work that has to be done."

Goldberg shared some advice with us regarding looking for a manager: "It's better to wait to find the right manager than to get stuck earlier in your career with the wrong manager."

A Lawyer's View

Entertainment lawyer Stephen Stohn is a songwriter who put himself through law school in order to learn about the business and legal aspects of the industry. He met Alannah about ten years ago, when "she was writing songs, and singing, and wanted to be a rock 'n roll star." Stohn's involvement was, at first, informal. Impressed with the demo tapes she and Ward were putting together, he helped her "shop" them around, sending them out to record companies. "It's hard to tell at what point it evolved into a 'professional' relationship," puzzles Stohn. It was Stohn, in fact, who convinced them to create a video to complement the three song demo that would get them an American record deal. His reasoning was that the demo was too good, a sure thing, and that they shouldn't leave anything to chance. The video, he said, would showcase Alannah, and answer the inevitable question, "What does she look like on stage?" "As well, it would set it apart from other tapes the record companies were receiving at that time. It wasn't usual, three years ago, to do video demos."

Stohn, of course, became deeply involved in negotiating the record deal, once it was established that Myles would be signed to Atlantic Records in the U.S. In getting to that point, however, Stohn stresses that, "Persistence is the key. Even if you have an excellent tape, it's so hard to get a deal. You just have to keep on trying and not give up. Alannah visualized what she wanted, and went after it. She would not be side-tracked." Record deals are generally pretty similar, explains Stohn. "You get a royalty of roughly a dollar an album, sometimes expressed as a percentage of the retail price, and sometimes as a percentage of the wholesale price. There's a million different ways that they chip away at it. The recording costs and half of the video costs are generally deducted from the royalty. So, if you produce an album for $150 000 and there's two $50 000 videos, you've built up an unrecoupable debt of $250 000; you've got to sell 250 000 units to break even. And so, I would have a conversation like that with Alannah, 250 000 is a good selling record; it's two and a half times platinum in Canada, and the record company would be delighted if you sold that many on your first album. She didn't even want to talk about that. She'd say, 'I'm selling at least a million!'" (*The album has, thus far, exceeded seven times platinum in Canada and platinum in the U.S.*)

* * *

Producing the Record

Producer/songwriter David Tyson has been part of the "team" for about five years. "There was," he says, "a lot of chemistry between the three of us." Much has been made in the media of Alannah's so-called "attitude". It is difficult to imagine that people like Tyson or Christopher Ward and, later on, engineer Kevin Doyle and lawyer Stephen Stohn would want to devote so much of their time, energy and faith, especially with no money involved, in someone who was negative, arrogant or bitter. "She's probably the most positive individual I've ever met," confides Tyson. "She never wanted to give up on anything. In the studio it was a case of 'do it until we drop.' It's a shame that certain people have the wrong impression of her. She's got a great deal of energy, and sometimes people misinterpret that. It would be great to dispel the rumour that she's negative because it's exactly the opposite. She's very strong in what she wants and what she believes in.

"I would hope that Canadian artists realize that with enough tenacity and hard work, combined with talent, they can reach the international level. Also, it's very important to be as schooled and prepared as possible. It's not a whimsical field to be in. Knowledge pays off."

Tyson stressed the importance of teamwork. "There's no question that three heads are better than one. Plus, it makes the process a lot more enjoyable."

◆

Insights and Outlooks

1. What does this article suggest is key to success in the music industry? Do you agree? Was there anything that surprised you?

2. Many potential superstars have been one-hit wonders, falling from stardom overnight. If Alannah Myles were to disappear into obscurity, how would you view her career? Would you consider her a "failure"? Explain.

3. What quality of Alannah Myles' character does the article suggest is sometimes incorrectly reported as "an attitude"? Do you think successful artists are subject to misinterpretation in the media? Why?

4. Do some research on your favourite successful musical artist or group. Discover how long it took to find success and identify the specific qualities that you think got them to the top. Write a profile of the star or group.

ON THE TRAIL

To me every hour of the light
and dark is a miracle.
Every cubic inch of space
is a miracle.
Walt Whitman

What makes someone volunteer to parachute into the very heart of a thunderhead or ride a fiery rocket beyond the edge of the atmosphere? What drives people to dedicate their lives to caring for orphaned animals or to saving the rich diversity of life in the world's rainforests? People have always tried to understand the natural world of which they are a part. It is a world that we sometimes take for granted, sometimes abuse, but most often admire for its beauty, its tranquility, and its vast power. Perhaps the reason that we want to know more about nature is that when we discover something of its character, we also discover a little of ourselves.

O WHAT A TALENTED
WEB THEY WEAVE

Robin McKie

**Spiders may make your skin crawl,
but take a closer look and you will be
surprised at how talented these
eight-legged creatures are.**

Next time you're cleaning house, take a close look at those spiders' webs
nestling in the corners before brushing them away in disgust. Admire
them for a few seconds at least, for cobwebs are miniature triumphs of
civil engineering, the animal kingdom's equivalent to digging a tunnel
under the English Channel or building a fixed-link bridge to PEI.

A spider's magnificent, diaphanous creations depend on one particular
attribute—the extraordinary nature of its silk. Unlike the silk spun by the
far more famous silk-moth larvae (Bombyx mori), spider silk is stronger
and comes in a variety of types. It is this last feature that allows spiders to

build such a stunning variety of webs, from the simple triangle of the hypiotes spider to the massive dense jungle created by latrodectus, the black widow spider.

However, despite the many attributes of spider silk, humankind has been slow to exploit it (again, unlike the silk moth's). Occasionally, webs have been used as dressings for wounds and sometimes for fishing nets, but in general spider silk has found regular employment only as cross hairs in optical instruments.

That could soon change. The genes that control spiders' silk production have been isolated and cloned by scientists, who believe they may soon be able to manufacture strands of the spider's microscopic yet extraordinarily strong silk in unlimited amounts.

It is not just the lightness and strength of spider silk that is remarkable. Professor Fritz Vollrath, of Basel University in Switzerland, notes that webs are made of proteins—a rich feast of nutrition that would be attractive foodstuff for bacteria and fungi. To protect their webs, spiders coat them in various fungicides and bactericides, Prof. Vollrath reports in *Scientific American*. In short, spiders use antibiotics, and it is probably for this reason that spider webs are renowned as a folk remedy for dressing wounds.

In fact, one of the most remarkable of all webs is made by the common garden cross spider (Araneou diadematus), the species that writer E.B. White chose to star in his children's classic *Charlotte's Web*.

The garden cross weaves an orb-shaped web that consists of about 20 straight threads that radiate from a hub like the spokes of a bicycle wheel. About a half-a-dozen of these strands attach the web to leaves, or to branches, or to blades of grass, or to whatever is available in an area in which spiders are seeking food.

Then a spiral of special silk is spun outward from the centre of the hub to create a fairly dense net. The overall appearance is that of a feathery dartboard—except that instead of darts sticking to it, passing insects are trapped there. The spider then eats them.

Prof. Vollrath says spiders also seem to have some sort of control over their silk production. "Some spiders can modify a thread while they spin it by altering its diameter, strength and elasticity," he says. "It is likely that they do this by controlling valves rather than the chemical composition of the silk. If radically different silk is required, they just switch to another gland. The female garden cross spider, for instance, can produce at least seven silks."

The resulting structure may appear simple, but research by Prof. Vollrath, working with Dr. Donald Edmonds, of the Clarendon Laboratory at Oxford, reveals that the garden cross spider uses some extraordinary skills to make an effective, two-dimensional web.

Most other spiders—like the black widow, for example—make thick, multi-layered, three-dimensional domes and funnels. An insect that flies into this mass of sticky thread simply gets tangled up and trapped.

The funnel web spider also uses vibrations to signal the presence of an insect, says Prof. Vollrath.

"Some threads are always stretched out of place and snap into a new position with a twang when dislodged. This adaptation may well have been necessary to ensure continued success at capturing dinner," he says. "In the arms race between web spiders and their prey, the prey is forever improving ways to avoid entrapment."

But the design of the garden cross's web is a much more basic form. It is absolutely flat, a simplicity that allows the garden cross to tether its webs to only a few blades of grass or some twigs. It is not dependent on branches of trees to act as anchors for complex webs and so the garden cross can hunt prey in open ground, which other spiders cannot do.

Function is diverse, Prof. Vollrath says: A web acts as "an early-warning system against predators, as a burglar alarm; and for a courting male, as harp and dance floor. But its overriding function is to trap."

To do this, the garden cross spider's single-layer web has to be particularly robust to withstand the impact of a flying insect.

The garden cross deals with this requirement in an extraordinary way. It makes a web out of plasticized silk that is essentially a form of reinforced rubber. The energy of an insect flying into this webbing is transformed, not into destructive forces that would normally tear the silk, but into heat. As the heat strengthens silk, the trapped insect actually fortifies the bonds that hold it. It is one of nature's most cunning tricks, and scientists believe it may one day be possible to exploit it, perhaps to make revolutionary new building materials.

But man has a lot of catching up to do. The evolution of the spider's web has only come after "many millions of years spent on research and development," says Prof. Vollrath.

"After all, if the recent interpretation of an early Cretaceous fossil as an orb weaver is correct, then orb spinners have had more than 180 million years to get it right."

◆

Insights and Outlooks

1. How do you react when you see a spider? Does what you have just read make you feel any differently about them? How and why?

2. Do you agree that cobwebs are "miniature triumphs of civil engineering"? Why? Can you think of other similar "triumphs" in nature?

3. In your opinion, will people ever catch up to the spider in the ability to weave webs? Why or why not?

4. Do some research on another creature you find particularly interesting or even disturbing. Does this creature have special talents or a special purpose in the natural world you didn't know about? Present a report to the class describing your discoveries. Include illustrations or pictures.

TWICE STRUCK

Michael Clugston

Have you ever wondered what causes lightning — that dazzling flash of mysterious energy that streaks across the sky?

Tennyson called it a "flying flame." Benjamin Franklin termed it a "sudden and terrible mischief." In Roman mythology, the god Jupiter used spiky thunderbolts as letters to the editor when he chose to show displeasure with the poor mortals below.

By whatever name, lightning is a spectacular natural event. Captured in photographs, its grandeur and beauty are safely petrified in static portraits of primal energy. In reality, at 24 000 to 28 000 degrees C, it is four times hotter than the surface of the sun. It can vaporize steel, plough up fields, shatter giant trees and scatter livid incendiary sparks over vast forests. Each day, it kills 20 people.

Its horror is the haphazard nature of its violence, a random Russian-roulette threat beyond control. If you are caught out in the open during a thunderstorm, it can look like the oncoming headlights of celestial chaos. Lightning can terrify you, charm you with its beauty, fry you or, prosaically enough, bring on asthma, drowsiness and other discomfiting side effects from the ionized air it creates.

Ask a scientist what lightning is, and he or she will most likely remind you of the electric kiss you get indoors on a dry winter day when you walk across a carpet and then touch an electric switch or another person. That nasty little jolt is the micro version of the heaven-sent tracery that can look as delicate as needlepoint while travelling between 100 000 and 300 000 kilometres per second.

But the scientist will also tell you that there is still a considerable mystery to lightning. "In some areas, we really don't know what's happening up there," says Andrew Podgorski, a senior research officer at the National Research Council of Canada in Ottawa and head of the Electromagnetic Interference/Electromagnetic Compatibility Programme. "It's very difficult to predict where the lightning is being initiated and how the lightning channels are defined. Nor do we know how a lightning bolt itself can grow so quickly to the huge channel that we perceive."

What is known, though, is fascinating enough. If nature abhors a vacuum, electricity abhors imbalance. Like water, which seeks its own level, electricity tries to even out the imbalance on charges between two neighbouring bodies by leaping the gap with a bright spark. However, when we see that spark in the form of lightning, what we see is not what we think we see.

The colossal structures we know as thunderheads are giant electrical generators. They occur when weather conditions create rapid updrafts of warm, moist air that travel high in the atmosphere. Furious updrafts and downfalls of water and ice particles create regions of positive and negative charge. Lightning can travel between the opposite charges within the clouds or between cloud and ground. The negative base of a thunderhead creates a positive charge in the ground immediately below and sets the scene for the gaudy short circuits overhead.

Majestic bolts such as that pictured here were probably preceded by a weak electrical spark that descended from the negatively charged clouds to the positively charged earth. The weak spark is called the "stepped leader," named for its rootlike branchings. Near the earth, the spindly leader intersects with a shorter leader rising from the ground to meet it. This creates a conductive pathway of ionized air—a bridge of ions from heaven to earth. The stage is then set for the real business to begin.

A few millionths of a second later, a bright channel of light and heat—a lightning bolt—leaps back up the bridge, but the human eye is not fast enough to distinguish the leader from the bolt. If lightning appears to be branched downward, it is because the upward-moving charge flows through all the ionized side routes established by the leader. It is the return stroke that causes most of the thunder we hear.

Last year [1990], Podgorski conducted lightning experiments inside the tip of Toronto's CN Tower during a thunderstorm. "I thought about Ben Franklin while I was up there," he says. "But the tip is protected by metal, so I didn't even realize lightning was striking the tower while I was inside."

Franklin, the Philadelphia Renaissance man, flew his famous kite in 1752 to prove that clouds were electrified, an experiment which led him to the invention of lightning rods. By 1782, the only building in Philadelphia that did not sport one of Franklin's rods was the French Embassy. One official died when it was struck by lightning that year.

Ever since Franklin's experiment and well into the 1800s, lightning, and protection against it, has caught the public imagination. For a few years, people could be seen carrying lightning-rod umbrellas, which lofted a sharp metal rod on top and trailed ground wires behind them.

While we may think of such a device as a silly momentary fad, it was a big step forward in understanding from the Middle Ages in Europe. Then people believed that ringing church bells in thunderstorms kept the lightning from striking nearby buildings. In this way, the call of duty sent hundreds of bell ringers on sudden ascensions to heaven before the curious custom belatedly became unpopular. The words *fulgura frango* ("I break the lightning") can still be found on some medieval bells.

We still cannot "break" lightning, but we can study it. Experiments have shown that lightning saturates the air with positive ions—atoms that have lost one or more electrons. The heat of lightning produces ions by searing electrons away from the atoms in its path. For some people, these can bring on a host of unpleasant effects. "Weather-sensitive people have reported insomnia, irritability, tension, chills, sweats, dizziness and loss of balance, migraines and other types of headaches, visual disturbances, nausea and vomiting," writes bacteriologist Julius Fast in his book *Weather Language*. "Many people report all sorts of reactions."

But whatever the folklore or science of the day, our perception of lightning remains rooted in the universal reactions of wonder and respect.

———◆———
Insights and Outlooks

1. What have you discovered about lightning that you didn't know before? Why is there still "considerable mystery" to lightning?

2. Which, if any, of the following descriptions comes closest to your idea of lightning?

(i) a "flying flame"

(ii) a "sudden and terrible mischief"

(iii) a god's device "to show displeasure"

How would you describe lightning?

3. Have you or has someone you know ever had a frightening experience in an electrical storm? Have you read or heard about such an experience? Relate the story.

4. Imagine that you are going to teach a junior science class about lightning. In groups, create a chart, mural, or other display which illustrates the various stages in the formation of a lightning bolt.

OIL AND
WATER

◆

Andrew Ward

**Imagine walking along a beach and not being able to
"spot a single bird or hear a single call
on the cold ocean wind."**

I got home on New Year's Day after a holiday jaunt back East to learn that a couple of days before Christmas a barge had been rammed by its tugboat off Grays Harbor on the central coast of Washington and had leaked 231,000 gallons [875 000 L] of oil into the tide.

The scale of the catastrophe crept up on people out here. At first they had no idea so much oil had been dumped, and then they thought the stuff would flow southwestward, away from the pristine beaches and sanctuaries of the Olympic National Park. But over the weekend the wind kicked up and drove the goo northward.

By the time I got to the bird rescue center that had been set up in a convention hall in the beachside town of Ocean Shores, people were finding contaminated birds washed up along the mouth of Puget Sound, and globules of oil were lapping the coast of Vancouver Island.

A normal oil spill, and we live in a time when there *is* such a thing as a normal oil spill, may claim 300 to 400 birds. But this spill killed about 4000 scoters, grebes, murres, loons, canvasbacks, old-squaws, auklets, puffins: the bobbing birds of the Pacific surf who gather in these waters for the winter. As of the Friday after I arrived, 6610 birds had been brought in, 3851 of them dead. Of the remaining 2759 live birds, 800 had either died from shock or languished so miserably that they had to be killed.

The majority of the survivors were murres. In the wild the murre is a vigorous fisher-bird, as regal and comical in its elegance as a penguin, which it resembles, with a black back and wings and a buxom, snowy breast. But you wouldn't have known it to look at the murres people were catching on the beaches and bringing to the center in bags and nets and cardboard boxes. You would have thought they were naturally torpid and the color of railroad ties.

The same went for the grebes: fierce and frail with their flat-top crests and blood-red eyes and long necks and beaks. And for the scoters: as livid-billed and querulous as Daffy Duck. And even, finally, for the few shy loons that survived long enough to reach the center, where their pens were shaded and hushed over with sheets.

Some of the birds were so contaminated that they had to wear bibs to keep from ingesting oil when they groomed themselves, and so in bibs they padded forlornly over beds of newspaper and rag in the jerry-rigged plywood pens that covered the convention center's half-acre [2000 m²] of floor. The Ocean Shores Convention Center may never smell the same again after a residence of a thousand defecating fish-eating birds.

Park service rangers, National Fish and Wildlife functionaries, and state environmental officials ran the operation at the center, but it was staffed almost entirely by volunteers: students, retirees, birders, bikers, home-makers. Few of them had ever handled live birds before. They were given rubber gloves and garbage bags to wear over their clothes. The birds had a tendency to empty out when you lifted them, but the gear was really more for the birds' protection, to keep us from contaminating them further with the oil on our hands and clothes.

Volunteers did everything from crumpling newspaper for bedding to tube feeding the birds three times a day with a protein gruel. The main order of business was getting the birds cleaned so they could replenish the natural oil in their feathers and return to the wild. But the wild was still too compromised, and some of the two dozen washed and banded birds that were released before New Year's washed up on the beach again, soaked in oil. Eight hundred and fifty birds had been cleaned by the time I left, but no more were to be released until the oil finally dissipated, and so they huddled and preened in net-bottomed pens.

The people who came here to minister to them became engaged in an anguished communion. The birds were not grateful to our species for their circumstance, and did not welcome our ministrations. They quite naturally assumed that each time we scooped them up we were going to eat them, and so they did their best to slash and snatch at us with their strong, sharp beaks. But it was no small thing to hold a wild seabird, and people who cleaned the birds seemed to become imprinted on them. Just as they exulted when the bathed birds were finally released in the holding tanks outside, they sobbed and grieved when a murre died of shock in their arms.

In the fluorescence of the hall the volunteers roamed the narrow paths among the pens, moving slowly, shushing each other like librarians as they passed the loons. But even though the volunteers were driven by altruism, they had to keep it in check in order to sustain the most likely candidates for survival.

I learned this lesson circulating through the hall, feeding smelt to the grebes and murres and scoters. The temptation was to try to coax the lamest birds to eat and to shoo the most persistent birds away. I saw more than one kindly novice standing by a pen murmuring and waving a solitary fish at some poor, hunched nicknamed stray.

But in fact, you had to pelt the birds a little to get their attention, and flip the smelt when you tossed it so it registered as a fish before it landed in the camouflage of newspaper and rags. And you had to toss a good many fish at once so the murres wouldn't waste their declining energy on shuddering, twisting tugs of war.

You had to be a little less aggressive with the grebes, or they would think they were under attack and sound a shrieking alarm. Both the grebes and the murres, when given a chance, daintily lifted the raw, thawed fish from the floor and tossed it until they could swallow it headfirst in a couple of outstanding gulps.

The scoters, being ducks, were always falling out among themselves, and did each other injury with their gabbling bills. They made almost as quick work of a smelt as their neighbors, but they chomped at the fish sideways, devouring it in stages. Though their bills are blunter than the grebes' and murres', the scoters were more valiant, and snatched at your legs if you tried to approach them.

All the birds looked pretty miserable at first glance, the murres gathered forty to a pen. But these birds comprised a kind of aristocracy of the fittest. They'd already survived an ordeal of contamination, hypothermia, starvation, dehydration, capture, shock, injection, handling, and imprisonment. The cadavers of their weaker cousins lay tagged and frozen in a locker, to be used as evidence in the event of a suit.

But even these hardiest birds were languishing. You can tell if a bird is dehydrated by the protrusion of its keel, and if it's anemic the inside of its beak turns bright orange. Some of the sickest birds lay apart from the huddled groups with their oily wings outstretched. You noticed them blinking their eyes more slowly, or holding their beaks open as if gulping for air. Some grasped feebly at the fish that was offered and then shook their heads, as if politely declining. They bunched together in the corners of the pens: some of them, I think, to keep warm, or maybe they had just followed the plane of a plywood wall, trying to escape.

There's probably no underestimating the intelligence of these birds, but it didn't do to patronize them. Their simplicity is surely more benign than the stupidity, say, of an oil company or a tugboat captain or the rest of our heedless species. Some suspect it may not have been the initial spill that contaminated the birds that eventually washed up as far north and east as Port Angeles but the discharge from other boats and barges that seized this opportunity to dump their waste into the water.

Before driving home I walked past the retaining tanks, where a pair of burly loons were paddling after their baths, and I headed out toward the beach for a stroll.

There were a few gulls and crows huddled high up the dunes and a couple of sanderlings trotted back and forth with the tide, but nowhere in or beyond the surf that rose almost a half-mile offshore could I spot a single bird, or hear a single call on the cold ocean wind.

I have always found beach walks restorative, but it seems that oil spills taint not only the ocean but our perception of it, so that even its natural sheen and luminescence becomes suspect. It is hard to imagine that any number of gallons of oil man can carry and count, even up into six digits, can compromise such a vast expanse of surf and sand. And yet I found myself second-guessing the reflection of the gunmetal clouds and peering suspiciously at the brown sand churning in the surf.

◆

Insights and Outlooks

1. What incident or image stands out most in your mind after reading this article? Why?

2. How did you feel about the birds at the rescue center? What did this article make you realize about oil spills? Do you think people realize the damage that oil spills can cause?

3. What do you think motivated the volunteers? How would you describe the relationship the volunteers developed with the birds?

4. Collect photos, articles, posters, and pamphlets on oil spills or other natural disasters that may have affected your area. Create a visual display to inform others about the effects of these disasters.

THE ELEPHANT
WOMAN

$\blacklozenge$

Amy Charles

**Daphne Sheldrick is a surrogate mother —
to a herd of orphaned elephants.**

Four baby elephants are trundling along the dry ground in the blazing African sun, their feet brushing up clouds of dust. They're just what you would expect to encounter on safari — except that the backdrop for these elephants is not the wilderness of Africa's vast plains but the flower-bedecked veranda of a neat house.

This is Daphne Sheldrick's "home" for young orphaned elephants in Kenya — the triumph of a remarkable woman who has dedicated 40 years to saving wild animals, orphaned mainly by man's greed or bloodlust. At the moment the young elephants are enjoying themselves, rolling tyres on to their trunks and playing together, therapy to ease the trauma of having seen their parents hacked to death.

The African elephant is particularly endangered by man's greed, thanks to its ivory tusks. Poachers shoot mature elephants, leaving their helpless young to starve. Like human toddlers they cannot cope without their parents. During the ten years up to 1989, the African elephant population plummeted from 1.3 million to just over half a million.

Daphne has laboured for years to save the elephant, as dedicated to her task as was Dian Fossey to her gorillas. But, unlike Fossey, she is a native of Africa; her father arrived in Kenya in 1908. She grew up in the African bush, and came to love the many wild animals as well as the domestic animals on her father's farm. Her first "pet", a baby deer, was given to her when she was just three. "We all had jobs to do from an early age, feeding the pigs, washing the eggs," she says. "I fed my deer with milk from a baby's bottle," she remembers with a smile. "And I realised even then that, if I neglected it, it would die. I had a succession of pets—water buck, impala, young zebra. When they grew up and went off into the wild I suffered dreadful pangs. The hardest and most necessary lesson I had to learn was how to say goodbye. Wild animals never really belong to you— they're just on loan."

Daphne was married twice, and has two grown-up daughters. It was her second husband, David, who died 16 years ago, who persuaded her to adopt orphaned elephants to see if they could be nursed through their grief and restored to health.

By that time, Daphne was skilled in raising all sorts of animals. "Once they went off they would return with their offspring," she recalls. "To them we were just part of their extended families."

In the first years of her elephant sanctuary, many of the young ones died. Each death was more distressing than the last. "When I was asked to look after orphaned elephants, my heart sank," she says. "Over the years we lost so many because there was so much we didn't know. At one point, David suggested it would be kinder to have them put down straight away when they came in. In spite of all my experience in nursing wild animals, the one species that continued to defeat me was the infant elephant."

Elephants are extremely sophisticated mammals and their needs, both physical and emotional, are complex. Daphne discovered, for instance, that baby elephants were unresponsive to many types of milk. It was only by trial and error that she discovered that a product developed for milk-sensitive human babies was the ideal elephant food.

From then on, discoveries followed more rapidly—baby elephants need three-hourly feeds, they can have only local anaesthetics, they need body warmth. In fact, Daphne often sleeps in the elephant hut, cuddling the babies and supervising their feeds. "I've blown their noses and wiped their bottoms," she states, with the stoicism of a practised mother. "I know more about elephants than most—particularly scientists. You have to allow for an animal's feeling, for individuality. Some are passive, some neurotic and some excitable. When you mother an animal, you feel what it feels."

She cites, for example, the fact that a baby elephant, however hungry, will feed only under certain conditions. "They have to feel comfortable, with their trunk nestling against something that feels a bit like mum. Sometimes we give them a little canvas pack, or they will fasten on to their keeper's neck or earlobe, armpit or face. But they won't take their milk until the tip of their trunk feels right."

If the babies will not feed unless a mother figure is near how must they feel when their mother suddenly falls dead in front of them, blasted by a submachine gun? Daphne says that many baby elephants arrive at the sanctuary in shock, having seen their entire extended family hacked to death.

The nature of the elephants' death is particularly distressing to their young because elephants are social creatures, and will help a family member or friend who is ill. One biologist recalls seeing a mother trying to lift a sick baby to its feet and screaming with frustration when she was unable to. When the baby died, the other elephants from the herd covered the corpse with branches and leaves, while the mother rocked back and forth. Often a bereaved family will return to the bones of dead elephants many years later.

"Elephants do have long memories," Daphne says, "and they go into a period of deep grieving that will often last three or four months, which is when the really intensive care comes in. You cannot force-feed them, so you have to try to persuade them."

That is no easy task when you consider that they must take ten pints of milk in just one 24-hour period if they are to survive. Adult elephants spend three quarters of the day feeding and can eat up to 225 kilos of food a day.

It is also very important for the elephants to have several carers.

Daphne recalls how, early on, "I made the mistake of allowing one to become too fond of me and, when I went away for two weeks, she died of a broken heart. I now have eight keepers who rotate so that each youngster becomes equally fond and knows them equally well. And they are never left alone—not even for one minute. If this happened they would be terror-stricken. They've lost one family and they immediately think they are going to lose another."

Baby elephants are sent long distances to be put under Daphne's care, and her love and knowledge ensure their survival and eventual rehabilitation. But, despite growing international recognition of the plight of elephants in general, the wider problems of their conservation remain.

Elefriends, the elephant protection charity, publishes adult and junior newsletters. For details: Elefriends, Cherry Tree Cottage, Coldharbour, Dorking, Surrey, England, RH5 6HA.

———◆———
Insights and Outlooks

1. Have you ever cared for a wild animal? Do you know anyone who has? Do you think it is true that "wild animals never really belong to you—they're just on loan"?
2. Discuss what you think motivated Daphne Sheldrick to save orphaned elephants. How does she relate to the animals? Would you feel the same way?
3. What discoveries about elephants described in this article did you find most fascinating? Why?
4. Write a letter to Elefriends, the elephant protection society, explaining how you think the problems of elephant conservation should be handled.

—♦◇♦—

TECH-MARVELS

What art was to the ancient world,
science is to the modern.
Benjamin Disraeli

What comes to your mind when you think of
technology? Computers? Lasers? Synthesizers?
What about the amazing pyramids of the
ancient Egyptians, the fascinating devices of
the early Chinese to measure the direction
and intensity of earthquakes, or Leonardo Da
Vinci's early drawings of helicopters and sub-
marines that anticipated their actual creation
by centuries? And does technology refer only
to applied scientific developments or does it
also involve art and creativity? There may be
as many faces to technology as there are
names for rock bands.

THE HIGH-TECH
ARM OF THE LAW

———◆———

Richard Skinulis

"Their day-to-day work is the stuff of the best detective fiction and they use rooms full of gleaming gadgetry, together with simple, dogged persistence and an experienced eye to find out *who dunnit* —and to defend their findings in court."

A few years ago someone started blowing up railway tracks during a bitter strike in Northern Ontario. The only clue to the identity of the guilty party was an anonymous letter promising more bombs. Handwriting samples from 240 employees were sent to the Centre for Forensic Sciences on Grosvenor Street in downtown Toronto, but no similarity to the handwritten letter could be found until staff at the center's Documents Section employed a new and deceptively simple machine called the Electrostatic Document Analyzer (EDA). The machine exposed indentations in the paper and, low and behold, someone's name, apparently written on the same pad as the letter some pages before, clearly appeared. As it turned out, it was the name of a recluse who confessed to the crime when confronted by police.

The EDA is just one of the new tools that forensic scientists are using to make life tough for criminals. Forensics is the science of applying scientific facts to legal (mainly courtroom) questions, and it is getting very high-tech indeed. Forensic investigators now use computers to compare millions of fingerprints in seconds, and lasers to lift fingerprints off things like rough wood or even skin. They can find drug traces as small as one billionth of a gram, and then use antibodies to find out what the drug is. Their day-to-day work is the stuff of the best detective fiction and they use rooms full of gleaming gadgetry, together with simple, dogged persistence and an experienced eye to find out *who dunnit*—and to defend their findings in court.

One of the main centers for forensic science in North America is Ontario's Centre for Forensic Sciences and these days the greatest excitement is being caused by DNA "fingerprinting."

Deoxyribonucleic acid (DNA) is the chemical compound, present in every cell nucleus of the body, that dictates inherited characteristics. It has been discovered that everyone's DNA is as distinct and individual as his or her fingerprints. Although the procedure is infinitely more complicated and costly than fingerprinting, potentially it allows investigators to compare any biological material—blood, semen, skin—to a sample taken from a suspect.

"It represents the ideal in forensic biology," says Michael Philp, assistant section head, biology, for the Centre. "But I suspect over the short term it will be used selectively for things like sexual homicide where, if you have proven the rape, you have proven the murder."

Essentially the process takes advantage of the fact that DNA can be "zipped" apart and "zapped" together. During a series of procedures in which the samples are taken, frozen, digested and photographed over a period of two weeks, the DNA is extracted from the unidentified sample and cut up with a special enzyme into its personally-distinctive lengths. It is then allowed to join with the known piece of DNA that has been made radioactive (so it will show up on a photographic plate). If the two pieces of DNA join, then you have positive identification. If they don't, you have at least excluded a suspect, which is what a lot of forensic work is all about.

So far, the only drawback is obtaining enough material. Semen is considered one of the best biological materials for DNA analysis because it contains spermatozoa with its abundant nuclei and therefore more DNA than something like blood. A single hair does not contain enough DNA but a forcibly removed hair that included a hair follicle might, especially if a new process, called "polymerase chain reaction" (PCR), which replicates the DNA until enough exists for a test, is used.

All forensic results are useless unless they can stand up in court. The legal breakthrough for DNA fingerprinting in Canada came in an Ottawa courtroom [in 1989]. A man confessed to raping an elderly woman after a forensic scientist, who'd used the DNA fingerprinting technique, testified that semen found in the victim had a 70 billion to one chance of being that of the accused.

Although DNA is the hottest forensic tool on the horizon, there are other more pedestrian but still valuable techniques. A good example is the somewhat grisly art of "blood spatter interpretation" (BSI). Discovered in the 1960s, BSI did not catch on big in forensic circles until about 10 years ago. Now the biology section of the center trains new personnel by hitting sponges soaked in expired Red Cross blood with various implements at varying force and studying the results.

The technique was used in the murder investigation of a Metro Toronto police officer who was bludgeoned to death with a hammer. His son admitted to the murder but pleaded self defense. A blood splatter interpretation at the scene revealed numerous tiny splatters within a foot of the floor with hair attached, and some minor drops higher up. Analysis showed that the initial blow was inflicted while the victim was standing but the remaining, lethal blows, were struck while he was on the ground. The bloody evidence resulted in a first degree murder conviction.

The center is an unusual mixture of high and low tech. The chemistry section has thousands of automobile paint chip samples on glass slides housed in old Kodak film boxes. A summer student is paid to roam the junk yards to scrape off samples of cars the center doesn't have. And scientists with numerous degrees will spend days sifting through garbage bags filled with debris from explosions looking for minute bomb fragments. But they also have powerful electron microscopes and analyzing machines (all, it seems, run by small computers) like the Infrared Spectrophotometer (IS), which shines an infrared light through samples of things like paint. The light absorbed by the paint is interpreted by a computer, plotted out on a graph and compared to thousands of known chemical "fingerprints" until one is matched. In use only a few years, this method was first used to nail an attempted murderer who had cunningly rigged the scene of the crime with trip wires and gas bombs to resemble an arson scene. His one tiny mistake was to leave some paint from his shoes on rug fibers at the scene. Too small to be seen with the naked eye, the forensic investigators found the paint with a microscope and used the IS to match it with the paint on his shoes.

Forensic chemists are also using an exceedingly sensitive method called gas chromathography. All substances dissolve at characteristic speeds and can therefore be identified by the speed at which they dissolve. Using gas chromatography, unknown substances the size of half a grain of salt can be analyzed. In fact, the method is so sensitive that gasoline *vapors* found in carpet fibers at the scene of a suspected arson can be identified.

Over in the toxicology section, machines like the gas chromatograph allow scientists to detect drug traces as small as one-billionth of a gram. The amount of material needed for toxilogical tests—usually slices of organ tissue or body fluids—is also shrinking rapidly. "Ten years ago we might have used 200 grams of liver for a test," explained section head Dr. John Wells. "Now we only need half of a gram. We are also doing things on a micro scale rather than the 'bucket' techniques we used to use."

The world of forensic science is a closeknit one, not only in terms of profession but location as well. Across the street from the Centre for Forensic Science is Metro Toronto's police headquarters. On the sixth floor, behind thick glass security doors, is the Headquarters' Identification Unit, which uses things like portable lasers that activate fluorescent dyes to "lift" fingerprint samples. It was used recently to detect fingerprints on a snake that was thrown into someone's bed in a murder attempt.

But it is the use of computers that has launched the unit into the 21st century. Indeed, some people may already be familiar with the results of one computer-driven program. Known as the Computer Assisted Recovery Enhancement System (CARES), it is responsible for the artificially aged pictures of children . . . who have been missing for a long time. Thanks to CARES the posters reflect the child's present appearance.

CARES is a software package that allows the police to make fast composite drawings as realistic as a photograph. Considered unique in the world, it was developed and donated by IBM when police artist Bette Clark complained to her staff inspector husband that it was taking her 80 hours to sketch an aged picture of one missing child.

Clark, a trained artist, sits at the screen to demonstrate. She calls up a blank face shape. Then, quickly tapping the keyboard, she inserts various stock eyes, noses and mouths, making them bigger, smaller, wider apart, anything. She also has a computer tablet and pen so she can draw on the screen. It is an awesome sight to see her totally manipulate a face, aging it, distorting it, altering it at almost hallucinogenic speed. "A realistic composite face can be worked up in about two hours, compared to the *days* it used to take," Clark says. "Then, a push of a button and 2000 copies hit the street. But the amazing thing is that in five to ten years, a lay person will be able to use the computer to age a person's picture *automatically*."

The system has other uses. Faces can be built up from just a skull, something that until now had to be laboriously done by hand with clay. Simulated computerized lineups can be created by surrounding a suspect's picture with computer-altered comparisons. Using the computer's tablet and pen, Clark can trace in the face of a bank robber (from a bank's security video) even though it is hidden by a balaclava. And bank robbers who wear disguises can be identified by distinctive marks like moles, or even the shape of their ears.

Of course, our fingerprints are the most distinctive aspects of our bodies. Fingerprinting has been used in Canada since 1904 and there are millions of prints on file. Imagine, then, the task faced by police when attempting to match prints from a crime scene with prints on file. In fact, the ID unit has a room full of people peering into magnifying glasses, endlessly comparing prints. But this is going to get better. Metro's ID unit purchased a $3 million computerized fingerprint database called the Automated Fingerprint Identifications System (AFIS). The system can compare millions of fingerprints in mere minutes. "You can have even a partial print, without knowing what finger or general type it was, and AFIS will run it through in minutes and give you a list of suspects in decreasing order of probability," says Sergeant Gene Pankewich. But, he stresses, "a trained human being still has to make the actual identification." Police are hoping that AFIS will boost the number of crimes that are solved through prints from five or ten percent to 30 percent.

While forensic scientists are arming themselves with the most sophisticated of weapons in their battle against crime, they are not infallible. Deputy director George Cimbura and two assistants spent two years doing little but running tests for the drug digoxin, suspected in the deaths of babies at Toronto's Sick Children's Hospital, and yet, their work has still not resulted in a conviction. It is the only case that produces emotion from the stoic forensic professionals. Standing in their stark white lab coats beside their coolly efficient computers, the investigators still grimace when the case is mentioned.

◆

Insights and Outlooks

1. Which aspects of forensic technology described in this article did you find most interesting? Why?

2. Discuss television shows, books, short stories, or reports you have read or heard about that involve forensic investigations. What impressions did these give you about the technology? Was it realistic?

3. Collect newspaper or magazine articles covering investigations in which forensic science is used. In groups, create a file of these cases. Afterwards, discuss your impressions of how effective the technology is and some of its limitations.

4. Use one of the techniques mentioned in this article as a key element in a television script, short story, or novel outline.

STEVE WOZNIAK:
INVENTOR

◆

Kenneth A. Brown

**"Whenever you solve a problem, whether it's mathematics in
school or an electronics project, in a way you're inventing."**

*Steve Wozniak had no intention of starting a company when he designed
the Apple II in the mid-1970s. He merely wanted a computer to impress
his friends. In 1977, however, he founded Apple Computer with Steve
Jobs. By 1980, their sales topped $100 million.*

*The Apple II may not have been the first personal computer, but it was
the first truly revolutionary one, and for several years it was simply the
best personal computer anyone had ever seen. Other early PCs were
largely tools for hobbyists and computer hackers. The Apple II, however,
went several steps further. Like other PCs, it could be used by computer*

hackers, but it could also be used for bookkeeping, word processing, and a host of sophisticated computer games. The Apple II's unique features —color, sound, high-resolution graphics, and high-density RAMs—soon became the standard for the personal computer industry.

Wozniak designed his first computer at age thirteen. He met Steve Jobs at high school in Santa Clara, California. They became an unlikely pair. Wozniak was the thinker behind Apple Computer; Jobs was the driver. While Wozniak designed computers, Jobs set about marketing them. In 1976, they got their first order from the Byte Shop in Mountain View, California, for fifty of Wozniak's first Apple computer, the Apple I. They built their first computers in Jobs' garage. To finance their business, Wozniak sold two of his Hewlett-Packard calculators and Jobs sold his Volkswagen bus.

In 1977, Wozniak finished his design for the Apple II, and the company was incorporated. With $3 million in financing from a select group of venture capitalists, Apple Computer Corporation began its climb.

Outside the computer world, Wozniak is recognized more for his wealth than for his elegant computer and circuit designs. When Apple went public in 1980, Wozniak's stock holdings made him a multimillion-aire. He has put his money to generous use since then. He has become a well-known supporter of the arts and of educational issues.

Steve Wozniak was born in San Jose, California, in the Silicon Valley, in 1950. He attended the University of Colorado in Boulder, and he later returned to the Silicon Valley to work for Hewlett-Packard, where he designed integrated circuits for calculators. In 1981, after a near-fatal plane crash, he took time off from Apple. During that time, he attended the University of California at Berkeley under an assumed name and earned a degree in computer science. He left Apple in 1985 to start CL 9, or Cloud Nine. His latest project is a programmable remote-control device for home entertainment systems.

INTERVIEWER: *Was there anyone in your background who really encouraged you to become an inventor?*

WOZNIAK: Tom Swift,* no question. He made it a good thing to invent and be a scientist. Winning science fairs at an early age or even entering science fairs was also important. If you enter a science fair and do

---

* "The *Tom Swift, Jr.* books were a series about an inventor that was popular when I was growing up in the 1950s. They were sold alongside *Nancy Drew* and *The Hardy Boys.* I can recall always waiting until a new one I hadn't read yet came out!" —Steve Wozniak

something well, you get a lot of positive feedback from parents and teachers and the like. In your head, being an inventor becomes a good thing.

My father also gave me some direction because he was an electrical engineer. When the right times came around, he helped me with electronics projects. He would stand at a blackboard for no reason at all and teach me about transistors. He helped me learn things that weren't even taught in school. He also gave me some of the first books on computer programming, even though he didn't program himself. So, he influenced me a lot and gave me direction. I kind of wanted to be an engineer like my father.

INTERVIEWER: What do you consider your first invention? Was it the Apple?

WOZNIAK: Not really. Whenever you solve a problem, whether it's mathematics in school or an electronics project, in a way you're inventing. Before I worked on the Apple, I worked on some electronics problems that were really kind of inventions. I built an adder-subtracter in the eighth grade, and I solved some circuit problems such as how to build a gate with two diodes. The two diodes wouldn't work, so I had to put transistors in there as well.

While I was in college, I invented my own version of a blue box.** In the three years just before the Apple, I totally designed a video terminal and a version of the video game Pong, which influenced some of the people at Atari who wanted to hire me. I also designed a movie system for hotel-room televisions back in 1970. Because I was interested in electronics, I was doing a lot of projects on the side even though I was working at Hewlett-Packard as an engineer on calculators.

INTERVIEWER: The early days of Apple have been described as a "ride on a rocket." Were you ever surprised at the way the personal computer market took off when the Apple was introduced?

WOZNIAK: No, never once. I designed these computers to show off to my friends; I didn't have any plan to start a company. I knew from my electronics background that computers were going to sell at least a million units, even when they had sold only twenty thousand. I used to have a ham radio license, and I knew there was a large market for ham radios.

** Electronic device that generates tones to "fool" and trigger telephone circuits. The original blue box was built by John Draper, alias Captain Crunch, who served a prison term for using his invention.

And I also knew there were more computer people than ham radio operators.

In the beginning it wasn't a big shock. It happened so gradually that, by the time the market became as big as it is today, we already were very successful and already had a big, successful company. It was then that the personal computer industry went much further than we thought. Instead of being a $2 billion industry it was maybe an $8 billion industry.

I didn't think we would sell as many as we did or that the industry would become as big as it is today. If I had, I would have based all the decisions on building a product that consumers would like and that we could sell. And, we probably would have made the wrong decisions technically and built the wrong product.

INTERVIEWER: What do you think it takes to come up with a good invention? You mentioned that everything converged for the Apple II. Is it just luck?

WOZNIAK: You've got to have a pretty darn good idea in your head of an end goal. You can't just sit down and start using some tools you were taught and see where it takes you. You need one goal, and your goal has to coincide with something that somebody else wants to buy or something that will save them money.

INTERVIEWER: Are there any particular traits that an inventor needs to have?

WOZNIAK: It's very good if you can spread yourself over several disciplines.

Some people get down to one discipline. For example, I designed a certain part of a tape recorder amplifier; I took that as my job. I like to do these one after the other, maybe ten a year.

But in my experience, it has been very motivating to be able to whip out a piece of software for this task, build up a language over here, connect these chips together. When you can transcend different disciplines, several disciplines, you can make things much more optimal. And this is what makes something artistic. You make a better circuit when you know what kind of code is involved.

Getting good feedback is also important. I had the best in the world when I was developing the Apple II. When I had something, I would just take it down to the Homebrew Computer Club in Palo Alto.

I was shy. I was really shy. I would never raise my hand and say, "I have something I'm going to be showing." I would just set it up on a table, and a few people would gather around me by accident. I developed my own group that way, and I would just tell them what I had come up with. And the look in their eyes was the sort of feedback you don't quite get from a boss in a company. They knew that what I had done was important, and they knew why it was good.

It's very hard to get that kind of feedback, to know what you've done is important. When you design a product for a company, the feedback is: "Now we have this product, and we're going to put our name on it, so it better be good."

INTERVIEWER: Negative feedback is also a problem, isn't it? One inventor I talked to said he never tells anyone what he's working on because people can be so negative. Have you ever felt that way?

WOZNIAK: Exactly, exactly! Right and left! Right and left! And I put up with it. I'm really patient and nice to people. But it's hard when you have an idea and you want to implement it the way you see it and everybody else tells you why it won't work. The funny thing is that sometimes they'll have very good logical reasons and they are right from some viewpoint.

But the trouble is that often a different approach makes no difference in the outcome. For example, I can use approach A, approach B, or approach C—it doesn't matter which I choose. In the end, the important thing is that I get it done. And in getting it done, the most important thing is confidence.

Anybody can point out a minus—"Well, that's not the way because it has a higher density of electrons," and this and that. The trouble is that it's not a fair way to judge an idea or an invention. Other people will look at a new idea and say, "Wow, that's great. Show me more later."

But it's a real problem when other people look over your shoulder and judge your invention before it's done. If you can wait to get feedback about a product until after you're done, you're kind of safe. You can take a whole bunch of lousy approaches as long as the final product is very good. You're only going to get feedback about the good product. People aren't going to know all the wrong approaches you took.

I can be judged on the outcome of the Apple. Boy, if somebody had been looking over my shoulder saying, "No, no, you ought to do it this way for that reason or that way for this reason," I know what I would have done: I would not have produced such a good product. The Apple had a rare purity for projects in this business.

INTERVIEWER: Do you usually work alone?

WOZNIAK: Anything that I've ever been proud of or was acknowledged for later was always done on my own. As a matter of fact, in school I was always very much an individualist. To me, a teacher or a classroom didn't matter at all. I learned by reading in my bedroom or dorm room late at night or whenever I wanted to. Sometimes, I would do a whole course in a two-week cram.

Alan Baum is about the only other person I've done computer work with in my life. He and I went back and forth on some of the Apple II design. He would suggest a direction, suggest some code to start it with, and I would do some improvements on it because I was a good coder. We would work together like that. But that was about it.

Otherwise, all my life I've done things very much alone—in my little apartment, at midnight at Hewlett-Packard working on my lab bench on Apple projects, or just sitting in my house all alone writing codes. Even some of the work I've gotten done for this company, CL 9, has been like that.

For example, I wrote one set of code release for a custom microprocessor two summers ago when my wife was in Europe with the kids. I don't like to miss my family, and I would actually fly over on weekends to see them and fly back to the United States during the week. As it turned out, during those three weeks with just enough time alone and away from the family, I got a ton of work done. I could go for a year trying to get done what I accomplished in those three weeks.

In general, I spend a lot of time on anything I work on. I have to sit down and work out a problem on paper, working it out very carefully until I understand every line, every connection, how to improve this or that. It comes out very slowly.

The process sort of starts, and then it may continue over several days. I'll scrap things together, try this, try this—with no one around. Whereas other designers come in, and—blip, blip, blip—they whip it out and it's done. And it's beautiful. But I have to think out a design in a way that I know is optimal. My whole life has been this way—every electronics project I ever did. I was sort of known for it.

INTERVIEWER: Do inventors and other creative people need a certain amount of time alone to focus sharply enough on the work to come up with a new idea?

WOZNIAK: It's characteristic of artistic people that they spend an incredible amount of time working on what seems like very little. Even looking back at my own work, I can see some places where I spent a ton of hours working to save one tiny little bit of a part. I can question the worth of my work from a business standpoint. How can I say it was worth anything? But it was worth it for my motivation.

I remember once that I designed a PC board for our disk interface. I did a rare thing for an engineer. I laid out the board myself. At Apple, we had departments that usually did that. But I came in many nights in a row, working very, very late. I laid out the whole board, and then I got an idea to save one feed-through. So I took the board apart, I trashed maybe a week's worth of work, and then I started over.

And I did it another way that saved another feed-through. No big deal. Nobody in the world would ever know that I laid it out to have very few feed-throughs—three instead of maybe fifty. None of this would ever be seen, but for some reason it seemed important to me in an artistic sense. You can have a feeling that all these things are important, but you can't necessarily justify them logically. The effort comes from being so close to your art.

INTERVIEWER: Rather than just work on something and get it out of the way, you like to come back and keep refining it?

WOZNIAK: Almost always. With any idea I have, I'll go through and work it out, work it out. After I've found one solution, I'll go through it chip by chip. I'll go through our manual and look for something that's going to throw an idea my way—such as a slightly different mathematical algorithm. Even before I build a computer, I'll do that.

Once I have several pieces finished—the code is written, the circuits are built, and so on—I might accidentally stumble across something in the manual, and an idea will click suddenly. I don't know, maybe my learning is subliminal. I'm sure many other inventors have gone through this before. You think it out in your sleep. I don't do it too much anymore. I've only had one night in the last two years that went this way, where I woke up with the solution I was working on. I used to do it all the time—up until Apple was so successful.

INTERVIEWER: Do you ever think of inventing as art?

WOZNIAK: Not so much now, but that's because I don't have time to do that now. I got hung up with a bunch of artifacts in my life. Back then, yes. I understood that it was identical to, or close to being, a musician. . . .

It's hard for me to think back now to why I thought that. I have to go back in time frames, back in time five or ten years when I knew. I can't even put it in its reality so that you can feel it right now. But when I was there, it was just so obvious that everything I ever read about an artist or a musician, such as the steps they went through, was exactly equivalent to mental steps I was going through. You know, the stages of turmoil and overcoming them to get a facet just right. Invention—like art—is kind of an idea that can't be seen, but you've got to express it some way. Back then, I knew I was like a musician or an artist. And I'm not right now. I only come close to it on occasion.

INTERVIEWER: It's said that some writers have only one book in them and also that some painters have only one painting. Do you think that's true of inventors?

WOZNIAK: That will be largely true for me. If you are ever known in history as a good inventor, it's also probably true that you made a ton of money from your invention. And with a ton of money, you can buy yourself success on future projects. Basically, you can buy a project that's worth so much, put a few million dollars into it, and then get the credit for being the one to pursue a great thing. It gets to the point where you can't tell where the inventiveness was lost.

Walt Disney created his cartoons in the earliest days of black-and-white cartoons. People started watching them, they became popular, and Disney made enough money to start a small company. It wasn't very many years later that Walt Disney wasn't even drawing cartoons anymore. He didn't even sign his signature in the film credits; somebody in the art department signed it for him.

I suppose I'm sort of rare now in my current company because I still do some of the programming and circuit design. I'm trying to do even more of that kind of work than I am now. I'm trying to avoid just being a sponsor of ideas that I believe in.

INTERVIEWER: What do you think the future holds for inventing?

WOZNIAK: Are you referring to the idea that it's all been done before? Oh no, no, no, no! It always seems like so much has been done, but I'm sure people thought that way in Rome thousands of years ago. I've never had that impression. There will always be new inventions simply because there's a need inside us to express our creativity and inventiveness.

---◆---

Insights and Outlooks

1. After reading this interview, what are your impressions of Steve Wozniak? Give as many reasons for your impressions as you can.

2. Choose something that has taken you a relatively long time to complete and write down the process you used to get the job done. Compare it with the way Steve Wozniak works. Do you agree with Wozniak that there are many ways to approach a job, but what matters is that you come up with a good product?

3. Wozniak describes his inventions as "artistic"? What do you think he means?

4. Do some research on another inventor with a partner. When you have finished gathering your information, develop questions for an interview with this inventor that you can role-play with your partner for the class.

THE INFORMATION TECHNOLOGY REVOLUTION

$\blacklozenge$

William E. Halal

Imagine a globe covered with an invisible web of intricate electronic information networks making it possible for people at vast distances to communicate almost instantly.

It has become a cliché to note the revolutionary impact of information technology (IT), but the real upheaval lies just ahead. If the number-crunching mainframe computers of the 1970s formed the childhood of IT, and the flowering of personal computers during the 1980s marked its youthful adolescence, then the 1990s seem likely to see the passage of IT into adulthood. John Scully, chairman of Apple Computer, describes the future prospects this way: "We have been racing to get to the starting line. The really interesting stuff begins in the 1990s."

A number of trends seem to converge on the year 2000 as a turning point when the IT Revolution will become the dominant force governing modern societies. Far more powerful computers will be available, possibly using light waves and almost certainly using thousands of parallel processors. This vast new computing power will be used to operate highly sophisticated software that allows computers to do the work of experts, learn, talk, read handwriting, and serve as personal assistants. The current growth of networks, cellular communications, and fiber-optic cables should form the basis for a common information utility spanning the globe. And the use of computerized electronic services such as telecommuting, teleconferencing, electronic education, and electronic shopping will change the way we live and work.

A knowledge-based social order is now evolving in which homes, offices, schools, and communities become interwoven into a web of intelligent communication services offering unparalleled opportunities for accelerating scientific progress, economic development, education, and other revolutionary changes.

Computer Hardware

The power of computers resides basically in their ability to store and process information, and today vast leaps are under way in these fundamental capabilities. . . .

Fiber-optic cables, used in global telecommunications systems

Stationary PCs will still be used in the year 2000 for technical work, but most people are likely to use small, portable computers like the "laptops" and "palmtops" now being developed. These should be user-friendly consumer electronic devices, almost like a smart TV remote control, connected to information networks through the same technology now used in cellular phones. Data, written text, newspapers, TV shows, movies, teleconferences, and a variety of other information could then be displayed in multiple high-resolution images projected on flat wall monitors. Other cheap, small computer chips are likely to be embedded in cars, home appliances, and other items.

The net effect is that "computing" will no longer be something one does primarily while sitting at a desk; rather, computers will be ubiquitous. Life will take place in a living landscape of interacting, intelligent machines that help us through our daily chores. David Nagel, head of Apple Computer's Advanced Technology Group, thinks this development will be "a real turning point in the way we live, work, and play."

Another important development is the growth of the information infrastructure. Integrated information networks will greatly expand the communications traffic flowing today on space satellites. The fiber-optic cables now being installed by telephone companies are expected to reach most American homes and offices in the mid-1990s, allowing virtually everyone access to an enormous range of information and communications services. And open-system standards like the Integrated Services Digital Network (ISDN) should soon make it possible to create multimedia systems that link together all machines, data, voice, video, text, and any other type of information into one seamless whole.

Computer Software

Currently, sophisticated software is essentially built from scratch, with thousands of programmers working many years at a cost that usually runs into the tens of millions of dollars. But in a few years, this method may seem hopelessly archaic, rather like the quaint way we regard the building of the pyramids or Gothic cathedrals. Advances in automated software production should soon allow a software designer to simply stipulate the logic desired for a specific application; the actual programming would be carried out automatically as intelligent computers retrieve standardized packages of software and integrate them into a working whole.

Alongside this crucial development is the rapid emergence of neural networks, which offer a fundamentally different approach to computing. Rather than relying on the brute number-crunching force of the old hierarchical computer architectures that used a single large processor, neural networks use many processors operating in a fluid, parallel networking mode that simulates the network of cells forming the human brain. Like the brain, neural networks organize information into patterns, assign different functions to different parts of the network, and can reorganize to adjust for failures of some components. . . .

The more-sophisticated qualities of neural networks, combined with more-powerful hardware, should realize the exciting applications of artificial intelligence that have been promised for decades. These include quick and cheap solutions to tough scientific problems, automatic management of the burgeoning capital flows streaming through the global economy, personalized instruction on well-defined subjects, more-accurate and quicker diagnosis of medical illness, and all the other tasks needed to manage today's complex world.

Software advances will also help individuals navigate the ever more complex maze of information systems available. Intelligent software packages are being developed that function as a "knowledge assistant," "intellectual robot," or "slave" working on behalf of its "master."

Stored in an individual's portable PC and able to learn over time the unique way each master works, thinks, and decides, such an assistant could handle routine tasks automatically, search for needed information, respond to queries, and perform other such tasks. This computerized alter ego is likely to be given a name for easy reference—like Sam—and could even fill in for its master at meetings, much as a capable human assistant may do so now. Apple Computer is planning to introduce a "personal digital assistant" in 1993.

Information Services

The big question posed by the Information Technology Revolution is, What will all this powerful technology be used for?

In principle, most of today's social functions performed in person could be replaced by their electronic equivalents. For instance, a number of "electronic universities" now offer courses via interactive TV, computer conferences, and other media; the University of Maryland's University College announced in 1991 that it will offer the first degree program conducted electronically. An estimated 34 million Americans were working at home in 1991, and interest in telecommuting is growing rapidly.

Other information services now being adopted cover the entire span of human activity: electronic shopping, banking, trading securities, political polling and voting, home entertainment, corporate TV networks, teleconferencing, electronic house calls by physicians, psychotherapy practiced via closed-circuit TV, electronic publishing, and even religious services conducted via computer conferencing systems. . . .

Because people are social beings, information services are unlikely to *replace* direct interaction; rather, these services will offer a viable *alternative* to the real thing when more convenient. Road traffic is badly congested in most cities and growing worse, creating great incentives to find other options. As information services become more sophisticated and user-friendly, they will increasingly fill the need for that option.

Efforts are now under way to achieve a better match between social norms and the new information technologies. A good example is the compromise now evolving between working at the office and working at home. Employers want to spare their workers long trips to urban offices, yet often they feel uncomfortable allowing them to work at home. One solution is the "telework center," a satellite office that allows employees to work near their neighborhoods. Pacific Bell has been operating two such centers in California for years, Hawaii has created a center in a suburb of Honolulu for use by employees of local firms and government agencies, and similar centers are being used in European countries and Japan.

New Dangers
The Information Technology Revolution offers enormous promise, but new technologies always introduce new dangers as well as gains. As we become deeply reliant upon information systems that are so powerful and complex as to almost defy comprehension, much less control, great costs must be paid in human diligence.

For instance, ensuring computer security, personal privacy, and protection against destructive intrusions (such as viruses) will require far greater care and ingenuity as information systems become more pervasive. Even small unintended failures can be catastrophic. In 1991, a software bug consisting of three lines of faulty computer code brought down the Washington, D.C., telephone system, effectively crippling the U.S. capital for several hours. How much more damage could be accomplished by a skilled person who wished to wreak havoc with the large information systems that run the military, airports, financial markets, and other strategic functions?

And as information becomes the primary resource in a knowledge-based economy, far greater attention must be devoted to its equitable distribution if the world hopes to avoid creating an underclass of "information have-nots". . . .

Perhaps the toughest challenge will be to develop effective means for finding our way through the looming avalanche of data that even now threatens to engulf us. It is supremely ironic that people living in the Information Age feel more, rather than less, ignorant: An overabundance of knowledge leaves us with a heightened awareness of all that is unknown, even as we struggle through masses of data to find the information we need.

But despite these drawbacks of the Information Age, remarkably bright possibilities lie waiting around the turn of the millennium. Human progress has been made very slowly and with great struggle throughout the long advance of civilization, and now a great surge forward seems likely as science and technology harness the power of information that has heretofore been largely unrealized. Whether we like it or not, the genie of knowledge is finally being released from its bottle.

---◆---

Insights and Outlooks

1. Brainstorm a list of all the ways computers affect you in your daily life. What does this list tell you?

2. In what ways does the article suggest computers or other "intelligent" electronic devices will affect our lives in the future? Do you agree with these predictions? Do you have any other predictions to add?

3. The article suggests that the way computer programming is done today may soon seem archaic, in the same way that the building of the pyramids or Gothic cathedrals appears archaic to us today. What does this statement suggest to you?

4. Travel in time. Project yourself into the future, to the year 2025. Imagine what a day in your life might be like if all of the changes you have just read about or discussed were to take place. Write a diary entry describing your daily routine.

THESE GERMS
WORK WONDERS

Doug Stewart

"We know germs as creepy, slimy, hostile little things that spoil meat and spread disease. But to a new breed of scientist, germs are deft and obedient slaves ready to cure illness, clean up oil slicks, even make delectable chocolates."

The U.S. Army has long coveted the silk of the golden orb-weaver spider. Elastic, yet five times stronger than an equivalent strand of steel, the silk would make great parachute cords, helmets and bulletproof vests. "Unfortunately, spiders in captivity can't produce the quantity of silk needed," says Stephen Lombardi, a microbiologist at the Army's Research, Development and Engineering Center in Massachusetts.

To get around that problem, Lombardi removed a gene from one of the golden orb-weaver's cells and implanted it in a common bacterium that thrives in his lab flasks. Soon, this bacterium began subdividing. "Overnight, you have millions of bacteria," Lombardi says. Stuck inside each is a set of spider genes. These bacteria now churn out the protein needed to manufacture spider silk. If the process were scaled up, the Army would soon have all the spider silk it could use.

We know germs as creepy, slimy, hostile little things that spoil meat and spread disease. But to a new breed of scientist, germs are deft and obedient slaves ready to cure illness, clean up oil slicks, even make delectable chocolates. This potential germ labor force has come about thanks to the biotechnology business. Ten years ago it didn't exist. Today it's a $1-billion industry. Princeton University physicist Freeman Dyson has predicted that biotechnology will change the world more profoundly than did the Industrial Revolution.

Dyson's enthusiasm is due to the ability of gene-splicers like Lombardi who snip and recombine molecular strings inside living cells. These strings map out how a cell will behave. They determine, for instance, whether a microbe will turn milk into yogurt or into cheese.

In the past 15 years, gene-splicers have learned to reach in and extract just the submicroscopic snippet of a cell's innards they need—cell parts from the lining of a human pancreas, for example. The scientists then reattach the snippet inside ordinary bacteria cells. The altered germs now have the insulin-producing ability of human pancreas cells.

Once a batch of doctored micro-organisms starts to multiply, it can serve as a full-fledged chemical factory, continually pumping out the desired product without error. Most amazing, the germs mass-produce perfect copies of themselves. A single bacterium can become two, then four, then eight, then a billion in less than a day. All that's needed is enough food—a standard microbiological medium—for the whole multi-plying clan to eat.

In the late 1970s, some 50 million animal pancreases a year were ground up for their insulin, which is used to treat diabetes, and rumors spread that a pancreas shortage was on the way. Today a unit the size of a small refrigerator containing genetically altered cells can pump out more, purer insulin in a day than a hundred pigs could provide in a lifetime.

"The vaccine for the deadly hepatitis-B virus is normally made from the blood of infected humans," says Dr. Richard Flavell, formerly head of research at Biogen and now chairman of immunobiology at Yale School of Medicine. "Handling large quantities of infected blood is hazardous, expensive and inefficient. But genetic engineering is changing all that." Using technology devised by Biogen, two pharmaceutical giants—Merck Sharpe & Dohme and SmithKline Beecham—now manufacture the vaccine in gleaming steel tanks, safely and bloodlessly.

The first generation of gene-spliced products—nearly all of them medicines—has been a trickle. The next generation will be a flood. The biotech industry is hoping eventually to make everyday products like antifreeze, animal feed and detergent by the tank load. Earle Harbison, president and CEO of Monsanto, the chemical giant, expects biotechnology to be as central a force in the 21st century as chemistry and physics have been in the 20th. "To compare the old biology to the new," Harbison says, "is like comparing a mule to a tractor."

One-celled bugs may supply us with cleaner-burning fuel for our cars. At the University of Florida, microbiologist Lonnie O. Ingram has engineered a new microbe that dines on the sugars from cornstalks, tree stems and other woody residues. The bacterium then produces ethanol or fuel alcohol. "Using microbes to turn crops into ethanol is nothing new," Ingram says. "Ethanol is the key ingredient in alcoholic beverages." But the natural microbes that distilleries use are fussy eaters. They insist on potatoes, corn or wheat. Relying on such demanding microbes to provide auto fuel would drive crop prices sky-high.

So with a bit of gene-shuffling, Ingram brainwashed his germs into eating the sugars from sawmill and paper-mill residues. They eat waste and excrete fuel. With oil prices climbing once again, ethanol could become a cheap alternative for the family car—and reduce our waste-disposal problems at the same time.

Douglas Dennis, a biologist at James Madison University in Virginia, has long known about a naturally occurring bacterium that produces plastic. Unfortunately, this talented creature thrives only on an expensive sugar diet. So Dennis has spliced the plastic-making part into a much cheaper-to-feed bug that is happy to eat whey, a waste product of cheese-making. Plastics factories, by contrast, must use oil as their raw material. A bonus for Dennis's plastic: every bit of it is biodegradable.

A microbe's appetite for scraps is one reason manufacturers find them so attractive. Even candy can be made from throwaway ingredients. Since cocoa beans aren't grown commercially in the United States, chocolate makers import them from the tropics at almost $1 a pound [0.4 kg]. But scientists have discovered a strange little microbe called *Rhizopus dele-mar*—a fungus akin to bread mold. According to Michael Haas, head scientist at the U.S. Department of Agriculture's Eastern Regional Research Center in Philadelphia, Rhizopus excretes an enzyme that converts animal fats and vegetable oils—two abundant substances—into something almost identical to cocoa butter.

Unfortunately, Rhizopus is hard to grow in bulk. "So now we're taking the gene from Rhizopus that makes this enzyme," Haas explains, "and transferring it from the fungus to a bacterium that can mass-produce the enzyme all day long." With plenty of enzyme around, candy makers could rely on animal fat and let the foreign cocoa farmers keep their beans. Candy lovers might never know the difference.

Some bugs are more prized for what they chew up than what they leave behind. After the calamitous *Exxon Valdez* oil spill in Alaska's Prince William Sound, the Environmental Protection Agency used some naturally occurring one-cell beasties with a craving for oil to help in the cleanup. Early studies suggest the bugs may have done as good a job in cleaning some of the lightly soiled beaches as high-pressure hoses and detergents would have. "It was almost as if we had brought in fresh rock," Chuck Costa, the EPA's project manger, reported after a visit to the site.

Often what nature's hard-working microbes can do well, a custom-made microbe can do better. Germs with altered genes may someday clean up an oil spill before it has a chance to hit the beach. Ananda Chakrabarty, a microbiologist at the University of Illinois at Chicago, identified bacteria that had evolved a taste for industrial wastes. Chakrabarty implanted the appropriate genes into a bacterium suitable for spraying. In powdered form, these new bugs could be sprinkled onto oil slicks that are just starting to spread. Chakrabarty even patented the improbable creature—the first microorganism to be so honored.

For the moment, legal restrictions have confined Chakrabarty's charges to the lab. A number of critics contend that sprinkling genetically altered life forms onto fields and oceans would pose a far greater danger than living with whatever toxic wastes already bedevil us. Biotech companies face a thicket of red tape in introducing new microorganisms.

But a new trick called "suicide genes" may act as a safeguard against those occasional germs that do turn out to have nasty dispositions. Inserted into a microbe's DNA, suicide genes will order the microbe to kill itself as soon as it has done its job. The order to self-destruct could depend on some outside change—darkness, cold or a drop in some specially introduced food supply. This way, bugs that eat oil slicks would die off before they climbed out of the ocean and into your gas tank.

Just 20 years ago the thought of microbes making spider webs, plastic or chocolate would have seemed like science fiction. Now such products may be widely available in three to five years. And scientists at Stanford University, Massachusetts Institute of Technology and other research centers are pondering how to put bacteria to work on some truly improbable tasks. They might, for instance, be used to manufacture very small parts for tiny "biocomputers," in which each electronic switch would be a single molecule.

No one is predicting that germs will ever be smart enough to compute your taxes. But in the next century, thanks to the work of today's biotech whizzes, these tiny creatures you once couldn't wait to wash off your hands will be the microscopic heartbeats of a new industrial revolution.

———◆———

Insights and Outlooks

1. Was there anything in this article that surprised, impressed, or puzzled you? What questions or concerns do you have?

2. What is biotechnology? In what ways do you think it might affect our lives in the future? Write down your predictions and share them with others.

3. Many people question whether genetic engineering or the altering of a being's natural genetic make-up is ethical. In other words, do we human beings have the right to tamper with naturally-occurring structures? Debate this topic.

4. Choose one microorganism or other aspect of the article for further reading. Then prepare a brief report including pictures or illustrations and present it to the class.

— ♦◇♦ —

BEYOND THE EDGE

**The future is a convenient
place for dreams.**
Anatole France

Can you imagine what it must have been like to
be the first astronaut sitting in a cramped cap-
sule being thrust into the vast loneliness of
space? Or what about suddenly discovering a
hidden cavern teeming with life never before
seen on Earth? People have always eagerly
accepted the challenge of exploring new frontiers. Countries to which we fly in mere hours
today were once far away and unknown; tele-
phones that we use daily were once a new
invention which excited the world. New frontiers soon become known ones. Some elusive
but compelling drive pushes us to extend our
world and go beyond known limits to the new
frontiers of our universe.

A REPORT
FROM SPACE

———◆———

Roberta Bondar

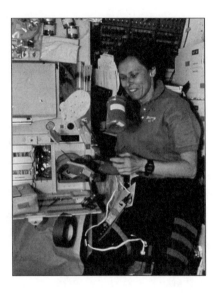

**"When you see Earth from space, it is small.
It is a planet to explore."**

Roberta Bondar was the second Canadian astronaut and the first Canadian woman to travel in space. The Sault Ste. Marie, Ont. native, a neurologist, conducted many of the 42 scientific experiments in the shuttle Discovery's cramped lab during the mission from Jan. 22 to 30, 1992. Among other things, she spun in a rotating chair in an exercise designed to measure effects of weightlessness on the body, assessed the spread of vertebra in astronauts' backs that causes painful muscle spasms and backaches and measured the effect of gravity on the growth of fertilized frog eggs. Speaking to Maclean's Washington correspondent

Hilary Mackenzie, Bondar acknowledged that, at lift-off, she and her six colleagues were thinking about the January, 1986, explosion of the shuttle Challenger that killed all seven astronauts minutes after lift-off. Bondar's report:

You sure have to think positively. We flew in January near the anniversary of the Challenger accident. We didn't make a big deal of it, but we remembered it on the launch pad. We were cheering when the solid rocket boosters separated from the orbiter. We had passed one of the dangerous milestones. It is, after all, an experimental system that has to perform in 8 1/2 minutes. And for that 8 1/2 minutes, we had spent hours training, going through the dynamics of the ascent. There were times after the Challenger tragedy when I thought of giving up. I asked myself repeatedly if I was doing the right thing. Was this the way I wanted to live my life? And then each time a shuttle went up I thought, "I'm one more closer to the pad."

As crewmates and as the payload crew, we had worked together over three years. For six to eight months, we had done bailout training. Our lives depended on one another—there was a bond there. We may have had disagreements, but the wagons circle when someone fails. It is a tightly knit group and there is a tight bond. We respect one another's strengths and weaknesses. I enjoyed the orbiter crew. They are really good friends and pals.

As we orbited over Canada, my crewmates joked, "We're going over Canada—boring. It's snowbound and inhospitable." But the snow brought out the beauty. It gave it different dimensions. The rivers were clearer because of the ice. The first time we passed over, I was playing a tape of *O Canada* sung by a policeman in the Soo. It was a pre-sleep time and I had the earphones on. It was marvellous—better than watching someone at the Olympics get the gold medal and see the Canadian flag go up.

My father died two months before the Challenger accident and I had mementoes from him in my personal kit. From my dad, I had a tie with shuttles on it, which I had given him when I joined the Canadian Space Program. From my mum, a locket that belonged to my great-grandmother. I had tapes—a tape for every mood. Tommy Hunter did me a tape; Anne Murray prepared a personal tape; and my aunt played the piano; I had a tape of the Girl Guides' camp songs and the music of [Quebec singer] Ginette Reno. I played Bette Midler's *From a Distance* when I could look at Earth and float before going to bed.

The feeling I had about the country as I passed over it was that I have touched that place—these people know that I'm going over and are thinking good thoughts. . . . When you see Earth from space, it is small. It is a planet to explore. . . .

When I looked at Canada, I never thought of a piece of the entity being separate. It was borderless, a continuum from sea to sea. There were no lines on the map or street signs up. I saw it as a united part, and I felt proud.

The most thrilling moment was looking at Earth. We can simulate floating, simulate science and see the IMAX movies, but we can't simulate looking at Earth. It comes at you out of the black universe. I saw the moon rise and set, the sun rise and set within minutes. It is the dynamics of Earth from space that you can't appreciate from the training or the photos. The science was great and you come back with a successful feeling, but the special part is seeing Earth. You can do science anywhere. Obviously, it's a tremendous challenge to do it in space.

It would be pretty dull if one hadn't taken risks in one's life. I feel the choices that I have made were not put upon me—no one put a gun to my head. But the main thing I've noticed as a woman is that we haven't got the free-flowing, easygoing network that men have. I feel I've had a hard time. People have had preconceived ideas of what I should do as a woman —preconceived ideas of my potential, of my behavior and of my contribution. That has been the limiting factor.

The mental attitude among some people is that women are not physically capable of being in space or that they are too emotional. If they *are* capable and are seen to function like men, then they are labelled as aggressive. I find that offensive. That, for me, is the hardest thing for women to deal with.

In my life, it has not been a question of sacrifices, it is rather the hardships I have had to endure. But I'm just going through life, going through one adventure after another. And if it had included marriage and a family, fine. I love children, and I am not anti-male. I was so busy in the last three years that if I had had a pet the Humane Society would have been after me. If I had had kids and a family, I don't know how I would have coped. I didn't put up iron bars around me and I wouldn't say that this life is for everyone. You have to enjoy life, and if being a biological parent is important, then you should do it.

If you are a professional and have a family, you need to have a support system. Society is getting too complex and is far too demanding of women to be perfect, while the male role has hardly changed. I'm not unhappy because I'm not married and don't have children. I'm delighted with what I've done. It was not a sacrifice for me. In the United States, women in the space program know when they will fly and they can plan their kids. For Canadians, there are not many flights—this was just the second in eight years. It is not as easy to plan your life when you are in the space program from another country.

The hard part was the three years' training for this and all of the travelling. It wasn't waiting for the launch. [Fellow Canadian astronaut] Ken Money and I had a phenomenal training schedule between Huntsville, Ala., and Houston [sites of NASA training facilities]—one, frankly, that was only possible because we didn't have young children. The three years of travelling was the least likable thing. We spent hours in planes and hours at commercial airports, unlike the U.S. astronauts who had NASA T-38s [two-seater jet trainers] available for their travel. These are the hidden costs. People don't realize that within the three years of training, constant travelling is the most tiring thing. I had to make my home here, have things around me like Canadian carvings that helped lower the stress level and enabled me to cope with the fact that I was not going home.

Now I'm going to give talks about what I have done in space and about being a Canadian on an international mission that was successful—and hopefully made the country proud. I hope the people treat me with respect. That is all I can hope. I have a great love for the country and a commitment to be seen as a person educated in Canada who has participated at the world level. It is the scientific Olympics. I didn't mess up. I have pride in that and now I want to share the adventure that I've had.

♦
Insights and Outlooks

1. What were Roberta Bondar's greatest challenges during the three years that she and the crew prepared for the launch of Discovery?
2. What do you think of Bondar's opinion that people "had preconceived ideas of what I should do as a woman—preconceived ideas of my potential, of my behavior and my contribution"?
3. Bondar's personal kit contained mementoes and tapes. If you were to go on a similar trip aboard the space shuttle, what personal effects would you take with you? Why?
4. Collect satellite images of Earth from space. Imagine you are an astronaut on your first space flight. Write a diary entry describing your reactions to your first view of your home planet.

WON'T YOU BE MY NEIGHBOR?

———◆———

Judith Stone

**Suppose NASA picks up radio signals from extraterrestrials.
What on Earth will we reply?**

"Hi! Nobody on the planet can take your call right now, but please leave
your name and number and we'll get back to you as soon as possible.
Have a nice light-year."

That's how I believe we should respond if Earth ever receives a message
from space; it'll give us more time to think. We may have to decide on an
answer sooner than any of us imagines.

On Columbus Day 1992 NASA will begin a ten-year search for extraterrestrial intelligence (SETI), sifting the heavens for artificially generated
radio signals. Since 1960, researchers have attempted more than 50 such
radio searches, but they covered only a tiny slice of space. Now NASA has
linked existing radio telescopes with newly designed computers that can
scan 15 million frequency channels a second—10 000 times more fre-
quencies than all previous surveys combined, at 300 times the sensitivity.

Astrophysicists think that in the visible universe's 100 billion galaxies, each containing roughly 300 billion stars like our sun, planet formation is the rule, not the exception. And radio astronomers tell us that the basic ingredients of existence—hydrogen, oxygen, carbon, nitrogen, brown sugar, and cinnamon—are available in deep space.

"If there is life somewhere else, the probability is vastly in favor of its still being in the blue-green algae stage that we spent billions of years evolving through," says Jill Tarter, leader of NASA's SETI microwave observing team. "But if they have a technology, the overwhelming probability is that it is more advanced than ours. That their technology would be somehow coeval with our own, a matching two-hundred-year period out of ten billion years of evolution, is fantastically improbable. We're the newest kids on the block who can play this game. So it makes sense for the emerging technology, ours, to be given the easier job—listening rather than transmitting."

And once the interstellar ice has been broken? Then what? A group of scientists and lawyers has created the Declaration of Principles Concerning Activities Following the Detection of Extraterrestrial Intelligence. Approved by the International Academy of Astronautics and the International Institute of Space Law, among other organizations, the document offers basic guidelines for confirming the authenticity of a signal and dealing with the world's press. Its final suggestion: Don't talk back until planet-wide discussions are held to determine what we should say. (Researchers are attempting to calculate precisely how long we might keep intelligent extraterrestrials on hold; they believe it to be a period slightly longer than the time required for an airline reservation clerk to pick up, but not quite as long as the interval before your turn on a cable-television company's repair hot-line.)

What on Earth will be our reply? Another international panel is at work on a paper suggesting principles and procedures for drafting a response. . . . Its suggestions will be submitted to the UN Committee on the Peaceful Uses of Outer Space. Then it would be up to the UN to decide how to talk back—or whether to.

"We have to think carefully about the consequences of establishing interstellar dialogue," says John Billingham, director of the NASA SETI program.

We have the right to remain silent—but we can't hide, Tarter notes. "Even though we might decide not to send a reply, our leakage radiation —radar, radio, and television signals strong enough to escape our ionosphere—makes us detectable." Tarter says it's unlikely that extraterrestrials will have deciphered the content of our radio and television transmissions. Still, I'm terrified that the first message from space will be, "We know you're out there! We've seen *My Mother the Car!*"

All kidding aside—oops, there goes my job; can we make that half-kidding aside?—two concepts must be made clear. "First of all, we need to dispel the notion that this is going to be like a phone conversation," says Billingham. "If the civilization contacting us is five hundred light-years away, it will take another five hundred years for our message to return."

Second, we must reckon with the idea that we may receive a signal devoid of content. Science fiction scenarios generally lean toward messages fraught with meaning. In Carl Sagan's novel *Contact*, for example, researchers detect a conventional electromagnetic signal carrying an encoded message-within-a-message that proves important for the citizens of Earth. (At first I was disappointed with *Contact*; I thought I'd bought a guide to installing self-stick shelf paper without turning it into a big wad that catches on your hair. But ultimately I got caught up in the book.)

Finding a mere beacon, its message too faint for detection, wouldn't spoil the fun for Tarter. "That will mean either we've discovered an entirely new branch of astrophysics—because as far as we know, nature is incapable of producing such a steady, constant, narrow-band-frequency emission—or we've found a signal that's been produced by another technology. We won't know what they look like or what they eat for breakfast, but we'll know the answer to the question, 'Are we alone?' I guess I don't have enough poetry in my soul, because to me just answering that question is more than challenge enough."

Billingham and Tarter think the time to craft a response is now. "I hope that the subject will be widely debated," says Billingham, "and that the content of the reply reflects an international consensus." I say good luck; in these parlous times I doubt we could achieve an international consensus on whether the sun's coming up tomorrow. But Billingham is more sanguine; he believes contact with extraterrestrials could draw us together in the same way squabbling relatives close ranks against outsiders.

We might turn for guidance to the official messages already forwarded to forever by the United States. The *Pioneer 10* and *11* spacecraft, launched in 1972 and 1973, respectively, included plaques bearing greetings, a coded map of the solar system, and a depiction of male and female earthlings. *Voyager 1* and *2*, launched in 1977, carried more elaborate tchotchkes: digitally encoded sounds and color pictures, and an instruction kit that tells extraterrestrial engineers how to play the record and build a three-color television receiver. Among the sounds sent aloft were animal cries, music, and greetings in over 50 different languages.

Tarter would like to avoid what she sees as unintentional biases in the *Voyager* messages. Some of the photographs, she thinks, could easily be misinterpreted by a nonhuman. "For example, a picture that we sent of a footrace in the 1968 Olympics shows a number of runners in the foreground and a stadium filled with spectators in the distance. An extraterrestrial looking at this might decide that it's a representation of two different kinds of creatures, big ones and little ones.

"Not only that, but the big ones are very strange because they seem to be bilaterally symmetrical from the waist up, yet they have only one and a half legs, and not always on the same side—these runners were caught in a midstride with their legs bent back at the knee and hidden. And an extraterrestrial might decide that our technology is fantastically advanced, because it's clear from this picture that we've developed an antigravity device—none of these big creatures is touching the ground."

Should humanity hire a ghostwriter? Billingham would offer no specific suggestions of illuminati whose input would be indispensable. "The SETI idea should be in the hands of everybody," he insists. "It should be widely debated by thinking people from all walks of life."

In that spirit, I scanned my fellow thinking Americans on several frequency channels; the following transmissions emerged from the crackle of cosmic background noise.

University of Arizona mathematician Carl DeVito admits that the scenario he envisions for Earth's first encounter with extraterrestrials sounds a lot like a bad blind date. He proposes that we reply to a message from space in a language based on the universal facts of science. "We wouldn't know whether they even have sense organs—but we'd know they have science. So we could, for example, present the periodic table of elements to aliens in simple arithmetic language, and if they understood, we'd share a common knowledge of elements and a common notation for them."

(I imagine the conversation, translated from DeVito's mathematical notions to English, would go like this:
Earth: Hydrogen!
Aliens [long pause—about 500 years]: Carbon!
Earth: Sodium?
Aliens: No, thank you; I'm cutting down.)

"Of course, we'll want to communicate about emotions and philosophy, but I don't know when we'd get beyond the facts. It's hard enough to ask a fellow human being a philosophical or emotional question. But with a language based on science we can at least ask each other about specifics."

Kids, I found, are enthusiastic about the idea of intergalactic dishing. Carrie Newell, 14, a freshman at Fox Chapel High School in Pittsburgh, is doing an independent study project on extraterrestrials for an English class. She's thought a lot about what to say. "We should definitely answer any signal. I'd tell them, 'Come toward us.' And if they did, then we should try to find out everything about their life-form and how it differs from ours and stuff."

Andrew Frisbie, a kindergartner at the Claire Lilienthal Alternative School in San Francisco, says that if extraterrestrials announced they were out there, his answer would be, "Oh, good!" (It's your quarter-millennium, Andrew.) But he says he'd consider adding, "What does it look like on your planet?" Adds his mother, Susan, an English instructor at Santa Clara University, "Of course I'd want us to correspond; to have our cosmic loneliness dispelled would be the most wonderful part. The message would have to be in some sort of code, obviously, but I'd want to say, 'Greetings, peace, and goodwill. We mean well, and we're curious.'"

That's the party line, but are we sincere? "The most fundamental thing one might want any other form of life to know is that we're here and we're friendly," says Diana Eck, professor of comparative religion at Harvard. "But are we? We're scarcely open to dialogue with people on the other side of the planet, far less different from ourselves than any extraterrestrial would be. In any case, I wouldn't leave a response in the hands of politicians or scientists alone. Far better to gather the leaders of the Hindu, Buddhist, Muslim, Jewish, Native American, and other religions. Each of these communities has its own sense of cosmology, of worlds far beyond our own, and a much larger definition of life than science offers. They'd add to any message a sense of proportion and humanity."

Koko, a 19-year-old lowland gorilla who has been communicating in American Sign Language most of her life and has the vocabulary of a six- or seven-year-old deaf child, thinks that we shouldn't sugarcoat our message. Says psychologist Francine "Penny" Patterson, who taught Koko sign language when the gorilla was a year old and has been studying and living with her ever since, "I asked her, 'What would you tell someone who didn't know anything about gorillas or people?' Her answers were 'Koko good'—that's always the most important thing—and 'People frown sometimes.'"

That was one of Tarter's concerns about the photographs on *Voyager:* They show an Earth free of disease, poverty, strife, frowns. I'd like to think Koko, canny primate that she is, wants to warn fellow nonhumans not to buy the hype of PR-conscious *Homo sapiens.*

Says Patterson, who has been involved in interspecies communication for nearly two decades, "It might only be fair for any message we send out to space to include a warning that we could be dangerous to another life-form, that we have already obliterated a number of them here. 'Watch it,' we might say. 'We can be shortsighted and stupid.'"

We'd better wake up and smell the cosmic coffee. Ann Landers has. "When that extraterrestrial buzzes my line," the advice columnist says, "I'd say as my first word, *peace*. That may be the most important word in the English language." And this confidential to Anxious in Alpha Centauri: "I think the word *peace* should be sung, not said, by Joan Sutherland or Pavarotti, maybe."

Many people mention music as a medium of reply. Says John Pike, director of the Space Policy Project for the Federation of American Scientists, "My favorite answer to this question is something Lewis Thomas wrote some twenty years ago. To paraphrase: I would just send Bach, but that would be bragging."

But Richard Muller, a physicist at the University of California at Berkeley, wonders whether Bach might backfire. "At first I liked this idea, but on reflection it scares me. You know how sometimes at parties people talk to strangers and they unconsciously reveal things about themselves— through body language, tone of voice, or choice of topics—that they don't realize they're revealing? Who knows what Bach says about us? Aliens could get a sonata and send back a superquark bomb to destroy us all because they *really* understand us."

(I think humankind is at once enchanted and repelled by the thought that extraterrestrials may be studying us in the way earthly anthropologists study "primitive" tribes—and may be drawing scholarly conclusions about our behavior. In Jane Wagner's play *The Search for Intelligent Life in the Universe*, aliens reveal to their contact here—a bag lady named Trudy—that after exhaustive research they've discovered that "in the *entire* universe, we are the only intelligent life-forms thought to have a Miss Universe contest.")

Thomas, in his essay on communicating with extraterrestrials in *Lives of a Cell*, counsels patience. "What kind of questions should we ask? The choices will be hard, and everyone will want his special question first: What are your smallest particles? Do you think yourselves unique? Do you have colds? Have you anything quicker than light? Do you always tell the truth? Do you cry? . . . Perhaps we should wait awhile, until we are sure we know what we want to know, before we get down to detailed questions."

Sunny, a college student who works at the copy shop on my corner, hid her face briefly behind a fresh Xerox. "With the shape the world's in, I couldn't explain us to a space alien without blushing," she said. But maybe that sort of accountability will be good for us. Tarter hopes that even the preliminary doodling of a rough draft will prod international statesmen to rethink their priorities and broaden their perspective—and get to work making the planet a place we can describe without embarrassment.

The Reverend Jesse Jackson's message would be, "Brother, can you lend us a dime?" An equally pragmatic Art Buchwald thinks the canny question is, "What's the real estate market like up there?" Children's television host Mister Rogers would give an off-planet audience the same gentle reassurance he offers his young viewers. "When it comes to understanding the great potential for good that resides within us, we are a primitive people," he'd tell them. "Those of us who are comfortable with ourselves are able to welcome strangers. Those who aren't, can't be so welcoming. Therefore, if you come to visit, you'll find a wide variety of us human beings trying to live on one planet trying to make sense of life and death and love and work and hate and joy. We have a long way to go to be the best of neighbors, but many of us are willing to try. Please tell us about yourselves. Do you know what it means to care?"

<hr />

Insights and Outlooks

1. Does this article convince you that there could be intelligent life forms elsewhere in the universe? Why or why not?

2. What are some of the problems involved in preparing suitable messages to send to our cosmic neighbours? What suggestions do you have to solve these problems?

3. The photographs on *Voyager* showed "an Earth free of disease, poverty, strife, frowns." Do you think that a message from Earth should include the negative aspects of life? Explain.

4. Make a list of questions that you would want to ask an extraterrestrial about its life and home.

YOUR E   S A
MIND   WN

Janice Dineen

**"Nowhere in the known universe is there anything
even remotely resembling the brain."**

So you think you're a civilized, reasonable human being? In the face of a
threat, you will examine all the options and do the well-bred thing?

Well, meet Richard Restak, the doctor who knows all about the beast
you really are.

Deep below the civilized layers of your brain lies the primitive limbic
system which hasn't changed in thousands of years. Human behavior has
evolved away from the caveman, but not this bit of your brain. The limbic
system is something we all share with jungle animals.

Here's what Restak says about the darker depths of his own brain: "I'm
certain that all kinds of chained and muzzled demons lurk in the murky
outer banks of my brainscape." The socialized parts of the brain live in an
uneasy truce with these creepy-crawlies, he suggests.

In a situation that feels very threatening, anyone may find the limbic
system rousing itself to create a panic attack, a sudden outburst of rage, or
a show of aggressive or violent behavior.

Restak, 49, calls it "the fiction of the reasonable man"—the theory that,
when you're under severe stress, your limbic system can mug the civilized
parts of the brain and take right over.

It's one of the thoughts that unfolds entertainingly in *The Brain Has a
Mind of Its Own* (Harmony Books), his latest book about the insides of
people's heads. It's a collection of 41 short essays setting out the most
readable of the things he has learned and theorized in his years in brain
medicine.

He's a Washington, D.C., neurologist and psychiatrist, so he works with
both the brain and the mind.

His mom wanted him to be a writer. His dad pressed him to be a doctor.
He's balancing careers to please everyone by writing books about his
medical specialty.

Restak writes about adventures of the brain that everyone can recognize, such as the state he calls information overload. That's when you have so many things to remember some of them just seem to fall out of your head. It's like a telephone switchboard getting jammed because of too many calls on Mother's Day.

When your brain's circuits get jammed with too much information, Restak says, you show some of the symptoms of information overload. You start out getting irritable, or bored and unresponsive, and you find you can't make even the simplest of decisions. Eventually you can be overwhelmed by a feeling of "so what?" about everything.

The only way to recover, he says, is to cut yourself off from new information for a while, because any that you hear will be disorienting and confusing. Unplug the TV and the radio, and steer conversations into restful areas. For self-protection, he says, free yourself as much as possible from the junk food of information—the material full of bulk and trivia but lacking in any intellectual value.

In fact, Restak declares, television news can be bad for your mental health on a daily basis. Reading about a personal tragedy or a natural disaster is a completely different experience from seeing video images of it. Reading sends the information through the part of the brain that deals with language, reason and logic. This helps to deal with the information in a reasonable way.

Seeing video pictures of it, however, bypasses the reasoning part of the brain and has an enormous psychological impact. "We resonate to it in the right hemisphere of our brain," Restak explains.

The fear, horror and outrage this can stir up becomes more than a person can cope with. To protect itself, the brain will eventually shut down. "Hideous images cease to arouse any emotion except, perhaps, boredom," he says.

Watching stark, shocking, bloody pictures numbs the sensitivities. It results in personal insensitivity to the plight of people suffering hunger, unemployment, pain and death, he says. The violence and horror on television and in movies has "injurious effects on our brains and mental health," he adds.

"It's okay to read it in the newspaper. That's a different brain reaction. But TV news changes our brain function." He calls its depictions of violence "obscene."

A person's whole outlook on life is influenced by pathways in the brain forged by the way you act and circumstances you live in, Restak says, making it more natural for you to react with either hostility or compassion. For example, Mother Teresa finds it easier to be kind and compassionate than to be angry and competitive because her neuronal pathways have been tracked into habits of kindness.

Others may find they have tracked themselves into habits of anger and aggression, and the neuronal paths in their brains now automatically send them in that direction.

"Lawyers, and others whose lifestyles are focused on conflict and dissent, really have to make a big extra effort if they want to do something gentle," he says. ". . . We know the brain works in the way made easier by the paths that have been set. Essentially, we are what we do."

"It's not impossible to change, but it's very hard."

People living in big cities are more liable to set neuronal paths of impatience, frustration, cynicism and anger, according to Restak. Traffic, crowds, strangers cutting in on you in line or trying to cheat you, and similar metropolitan scenes from daily life can take their toll on the structure of the brain.

Studies also suggest that a gentle, loving environment has a positive impact on the brain, he says, and history tells us the same thing.

People are defined by their actions, though, not by their thoughts, Restak observes. Everyone has things they don't want to think about, and everyone finds these thoughts dancing up to the surface, teasing and tormenting from time to time. Health issues, fears about the past and future, difficult relationships, money problems, worries about physical appearance, and rejection and loneliness are some common ones.

The more you try to control and banish these thoughts, the more it ends up causing you mental anguish. In a mild form, this means that the more you struggle to try to get to sleep, the more likely you are to toss and turn all night. In more severe forms, the struggle to eliminate unwanted thoughts can lead to some kinds of mental illness such as depression or severe obsession.

The answer Restak offers is deciding to accept whatever thoughts arise in the disturbing area and willingly giving them room in your head. This denies them the status of unwanted thoughts, robs them of their power and gives you a new feeling of freedom. Eventually, he says, you become bored by the thoughts and they no longer arise.

One of the most uplifting messages in Restak's book is that it's possible to deliberately become smarter. "There's no question about that," he states. He writes that activities, habits and interests not only define personalities, but also affect the physical structure of our brains.

It's not necessarily true that the bigger your brain, or the more brain cells you have, the smarter you are. Someone with a smaller brain and fewer brain cells may actually have a higher intellectual function than another person with a big brain and lots more brain cells. Charlemagne had a bigger brain than Einstein, but Einstein had the greater intellectual gift.

The key seems to be how numerous and intricate your brain cell networks are, even the cells that are far away from each other. And you can improve your networks by enriching your environment, interests and activities. By developing new talents and taking up new interests, Restak says, you can literally change your brain for the better.

New information and new abilities can stimulate improvement in the brain at any time of life, including old age.

---◆---

Insights and Outlooks

1. What new ideas about the brain did you discover from this article? Would you say that these discoveries are all proven facts or are some speculation? What is the difference?

2. Have you ever experienced information overload? What do you do to cope? What are Restak's suggestions for dealing with your brain's circuits getting jammed with too much information?

3. Do you agree that:

a) violence and horror on television and in movies have injurious effects on our brains and mental health?

b) a gentle, loving environment has a positive impact on the brain?

c) it is possible to deliberately become "smarter"?

4. Make a chart outlining different situations, what you felt, and how you acted. Include times when you were angry, frustrated, and upset as well as times when you were comfortable and relaxed. Does your chart support Restak's idea that "we are what we do"?

THE CAVERN OF
LITTLE MONSTERS

———◆———

David Van Biema, Steven Petrow, Tala Skari

**What could we possibly find in the dark depths of a cavern
—depths never before explored by humankind?**

This cave, a mile [1.6 km] inland from the Romanian shore of the Black Sea, is a place that at first glance—certainly at first sniff—reminds people of hell. Even Cristian Lascu, its discoverer and in whose honor one of its more venomous spiders is named, describes the odor that assaulted him when he first journeyed down into it as "the hell smell."

The air in the inner chambers is lethally low in oxygen. The hydrogen sulfide in the water corrodes metal within minutes. Bacterial goo coats every surface. And then there are the tenants: a millipede with no eyes, only sockets; a crustacean with antennae like Salvador Dalí's mustache and the pallor of a vampire's victim; a tiny spider that *is* a vampire, sucking the innards out of its neighbors. Serban Sarbu, a biologist who has spent more time here underwater than anyone, calls it *"dezgustatoar."* Nasty.

But he says it fondly. For since its discovery, other adjectives have been applied to this place Romanians call the Movile grotto. *Fascinat* was the reaction of the professors at the Emil Racovita Speleological Institute in Bucharest when they began to get a look at its little monsters.

And then, as word got out to a few scientists overseas, another adjective: *Istoric*. Historic.

The revelation resulted from a dictator's whim. Three and a half years before his fatal fall in 1989, Nicolae Ceaușescu decided to build a nuclear power plant on the Dobrogea Plateau near the resort town of Mangalia. Ceaușescu, goes the story, gazed out a helicopter window, found the grassy seaside landscape below good, and pointed.

Some months later, workers drilling a foundation in the limestone came to a halt. Sixty feet [18 m] down was a large crevasse: a small irregularity or a project-threatening cavern? Lascu, a geologist with caving expertise, shinnied down the shaft to find out. Peering into an opening about

18 inches [46 cm] wide, he realized he had stumbled across something exciting.

He tore away at the opening with his hands, enlarging it enough to enter a narrow tunnel, which, after 300 feet [91 m], ended at a small lake. There Lascu was assaulted by a stench like rotten eggs, and he noticed that the water was mysteriously warm. He became woozy; there was very little oxygen. He barely had the breath to climb back to the surface and gasp, "There's a cave under your thermonuclear plant."

The plant was scrapped. Lascu was quietly overjoyed. He returned with some colleagues, notably Sarbu, a cave expert. Using scuba gear, Sarbu mapped out a long, often water-filled corridor connecting a series of air bells. In each successive bell, oxygen dwindled and toxic gases increased; by the last, the air was poisonous to most forms of life. The water was heated to 68°F [20°C] by geothermal springs and topped with a yellow scum, "like when you buy bad milk and see a skin floating on the surface," says Sarbu, who found himself wearing it when he emerged from the pools. As for the cave walls, they were alive with animals.

The first things researchers noticed were spiders. "Small and large," says Lascu. "Everything was moving fast, and they were all over the place." A geologist picked three at random and was astonished when biologists at the Racovita Institute declared each an undiscovered species. Next came centipedes, leeches, tiny crustaceans and sow bugs. All were shorter than four inches [10 cm], all were breathing levels of carbon dioxide that would kill their cousins on the surface, and nine out of 10 had not been seen before by humans.

Istoric. As mankind intrudes on the world's last truly wild areas, it is common to encounter new plants and animals. But to unearth an entire ecosystem of new species (27 so far) is unparalleled.

Not that the creepy-crawlies aren't fantastic individually. A leech yet to be given a scientific name sucks not blood but earthworms, whole, like a kid with a strand of spaghetti. A water scorpion lurks below the pool's surface, breathing through a "snorkel" extended from its abdomen. A centipede captures prey with its oversize back feet, which then detach so it can spin around and dine frontally. Even the majority of the cave's minuscule snails and crustaceans, if not quite so bizarre, have proved to be unique.

And they have been down there a very long time. Most species, after 100 000 or more generations in the dark, lose their protective pigment: Coloration in the Movile ranges from light brown to translucent. Nor is there much use for eyes: Some animals have fewer than their aboveground cousins, some empty sockets and others just an optic nerve. To compensate, many have developed long antennae and other sensory extremities: Wilt Chamberlain limbs on Martin Short torsos.

Most remarkable, though, is the food chain in which these creatures are arranged. From the top, it seems quite conventional. Large predators, such as centipedes and water scorpions, eat smaller millipedes and snails, which eat tiny fungi and bacteria. The extraordinary link is the bottom one. A bacterium, with the Latin name *Beggiatoa*, does not do what building blocks of food everywhere else do: It does not convert solar energy into food via chlorophyll and photosynthesis. Instead, performing a function it developed who knows how many eons ago, *Beggiatoa* makes food with energy derived from the separation of hydrogen and sulfide ions. In fact, the yellow color of the bacterial

One of the unusual creatures found in the cave: an aquatic isopod (crustacean).

scum that draped Sarbu resulted from tiny granules of pure sulfur that are a by-product of the process.

This alternative energy system may be well suited to the cave's midnight world, but it is exceedingly rare. The only other known non-photosynthetic food chain exists 12,000 feet [3660 m] deep in the ocean, surrounding jets of scalding water rich in hydrogen sulfide. But the deep-sea ecosystem is not pristine: Edible matter constantly floats down from the chlorophyll-based system above. And although a few caves similar to Movile have been discovered, the Romanian cavern is by far the least contaminated ever encountered.

For a while, this amazing find was neglected during convulsions in the political ecosystem upstairs. In early 1987 impoverished locals who had heard that Movile harbored "scientific treasure" vandalized the shaft's guard doors. Sarbu defected to the United States in mid-1987 because of persecution by government officials, and Lascu found himself blacklisted by the Ceaușescu regime because of contacts with American scientists. In December 1989 came Romania's revolution.

When the smoke cleared, the scientists returned, this time with American and French colleagues. Their working theory: Since the closest relatives of many of the cave's creatures can be found in the tropics, their ancestors must have entered the cave some 5.5 million years ago—during the Miocene Epoch, the last time Romania had a balmy climate. As the new immigrants thrived in their wet, warm grotto, no less than 17 ice ages drove out—or wiped out—their aboveground kin. In the Quaternary Age, centuries of winds blew clay dust over the area, eventually sealing the cave. From at least 10 000 B.C. on, nothing from the surface—new bugs, runoff water or even fallout from Chernobyl that has been found in nearby water tables—was able to penetrate the Movile.

It was, in effect, a limestone safe-deposit box that some experts now maintain safeguards a clue to life's origins. Earth's climate at the geological instant when matter became animate could not have supported oxygen-based photosynthesis. In fact, a sulfide-rich atmosphere is much closer to what might have been. *Beggiatoa*, therefore, may be much closer than green algae to the earliest link on the food chain. And some of the creepy-crawlies would be much closer than . . . well, Thomas Kane, a University of Cincinnati biologist, says that "going into the cave is like going back to Europe to see where your grandparents lived, who they were and the kind of world they lived in. Only this is going a little further." It makes one look more affectionately at that disgusting centipede.

It also increases one's awareness of the fragility of the cave. The intoxication of discovery has been tempered by more sober concerns of preservation. Cold, dry air from the surface has already forced some animals further into the grotto's recesses. Conventional species wandering down could also destroy the priceless little kingdom, depriving us of our looking glass into the way we were. Painfully aware of this, the Romanians have equipped the doors to the cave with airtight seals and are allowing only three researchers regular access. Even though they believe the cave continues beyond the known air bells, no one wants to risk what exists by exploring further. "It's a window, a keyhole into a kind of system lost in space and time," says Lascu. Adds Sarbu: "We need to make every effort to preserve it as it is. If we destroy it, there will be nothing to study."

And so a tiny hell is revealed as a miniature Eden, with mankind, looking down at it from above, responsible for preventing its fall. *Fascinat.*

◆

Insights and Outlooks

1. Why is this cave such an important and astounding discovery? How would you describe it to someone who knew nothing about it?

2. Draw a diagram of the unusual food chain in this cave. How is it different from the usual food chains in the world above it? What clues might it hold to understanding life's origins?

3. Scientists are very concerned about preserving this cave. Why? What steps do you think should be taken to protect it? What might have to be sacrificed?

4. Imagine you could put on scuba gear and go down into the depths of this cave, discovering it for the first time. Write a description of your experience.

—◆◇◆—

MORE TO DISCOVER

**Far away there in the sunshine are my highest
aspirations. I may not reach them, but I can look up
and see their beauty, believe in them,
and try to follow where they lead.**

Louisa May Alcott

Life is a continual quest for discovery. We can
look to our past for insights and to our future
for possibilities. In our present, we find the
immediate challenges that must be met if our
journey is to be successful. Some of these challenges will be personal. Others will be global.
How we meet them is what makes the discovery interesting. There are so many areas to
explore and in each one we may find new
sparks of insight and new connections. This
section allows you to browse—to choose
where you would like to discover more.

WHAT MAKES GOOD
SCIENCE FICTION?

Isaac Asimov

Wonder Woman or the Bionic Woman:
Who you gonna call?

Foreword

I'm not a critic (it's no secret that I am not overly fond of critics and reviewers), and I never willingly take up the role of criticism, of weighing virtues and shortcomings, and of making lordly pronouncements.

At times, however, I am asked for my opinion and sometimes I just can't resist trying to correct what seem to me to be obvious flaws. I try not to discuss literary values, concerning which I know very little, but I do have some opinions on the merits and demerits of science fiction that involve other aspects of the art.

What Makes Good Science Fiction?

The phenomenal success of *Star Wars* could not help but initiate a new wave of science fiction in the movies and in TV, and the first drenchings have already washed over our television screens. It is inevitable that along with the good comes the bad, and in the case of science fiction, at least, the bad is horrible.

Why is that? What makes some science fiction bad?

In considering a piece of science fiction writing, the first rule is that if it is bad fiction, it is bad science fiction. There is no magic that can convert something bad into something good just because it is science fiction.

The reverse is not true, however. A piece of science fiction writing may be good fiction and yet bad science fiction.

There is an extra ingredient required by science fiction that makes literary and dramatic virtue not entirely sufficient. There must, in addition, be some indication that the writer knows science.

This does not mean that the science has to be detailed and stultifying; there need only be casual references—but the references must be correct. Nor does it mean that the writer cannot take liberties—but he must know what liberties he can take and how he can justify them without sounding like an ignoramus.

It may be that most of the audience knows so little science that they wouldn't recognize ignorance if they saw or heard it, or care either. That doesn't matter. I am not trying to define what makes a science fiction show popular or successful, but what makes it good. It is perfectly possible for a dreadful science fiction show (or a dreadful *anything* show) to make a lot of money, but that doesn't make it one whit less dreadful; it simply tells us something about the audience.

Let's take some examples.

I enjoyed *Star Wars*. It is deliberately campy and it is utterly brainless, but the special effects are fun and it is restful sometimes to park one's brain outside. One can even forgive the kind of slip that makes "parsec" a unit of speed rather than of distance, and consider it the equivalent of a typographical error.

But—The most popular scene in the picture involves numerous extraterrestrials gathered round a bar, drinking. It is the interplanetary equivalent of the ask-no-questions-and-no-holds-barred saloon in many Westerns. As a deliberate satire on these Western bars, it is funny, and we must admire the imagination of the makeup artists in creating the different beings.

However, are all these strange beings perfectly at home in a single atmosphere, at a single temperature and pressure? Should some not find an environment insufferable that others find comfortable?

It might spoil the fun if such a complication had to be introduced and it could, after all, be supposed that all these creatures just happened to find an Earth-type atmosphere endurable. That would violate no scientific law, only the rules of probability.

Yet one of these creatures might have had to wear a space suit, or might have had to keep sniffing at a gas cylinder or ducking its head into a bowl of water. It would have meant very little trouble and would have made the scene much better science fiction.

Consider, in contrast, the television science fiction show "Logan's Run." Some of the people working for it worked for "Star Trek," so it's not surprising that its attitude toward science shows promise.

In one episode, for instance, an extraterrestrial spaceship is picking up samples of the dominant species from different worlds. They have just picked up our hero and heroine, and on the ship are also several pairs of extraterrestrials who have been picked up on their own planets. One pair is in a cage that is filled with an atmosphere that they can breathe but which is poisonous to human beings. This is good science fiction, and it is satisfactory to have it made pertinent to the plot.

Consider another point from the same show. In recent years, there has arisen the illiterate fancy that the word "galaxy" refers to anything that is not in our own Solar system. Everyone and everything "comes from a different galaxy." (This is like supposing that everything that does not come from our own town comes from a different continent.)

In "Logan's Run," however, one of the characters refers to extraterrestrials as being "from another Solar system" and a great peace descended on me. At least the writer knows what a galaxy is and is not.

There is no such effort made in "The Man from Atlantis." The core of the plot involves a creature (manlike, but a nonhuman species) who can live under water and who has webbed hands and feet. We can accept that as given.

In one episode, Victor Buono, as the unctuously comic villain, is melting the Earth's ice caps by a microwave device in order to raise the sea level and "attract attention."

The energy required to melt the ice caps as rapidly as he is described as doing it would be utterly prohibitive. It would take centuries to melt the ice caps under any rational human-made urgings and, once partial melting had taken place, it would take centuries to persuade the water to refreeze.

There is almost an understanding of this. The villain gets the hero to cooperate by saying he has ceased the melting process and shows faked movies to indicate the sea level is receding. After a long time, the hero suddenly realizes that the sea level wouldn't recede once the process is stopped. The excess of water must evaporate first, he says. (That's right, and it must refreeze in the polar regions, which would take a long, long time.) He therefore knows that Buono has faked the pictures and in his anger he does what he should have done at the very start—he destroys the microwave equipment with his mental powers.

And, of course, the instant the equipment is destroyed, the sea level *does* recede. —Unbearably bad science fiction!

Even children's programs must not show scientific ignorance—they least of all, in fact. On Saturday mornings, there is "Space Academy" and in one particular half-hour segment, two ships pass through a black hole, and later return.

There isn't a single sign, however, that anyone connected with the show knows one single thing about black holes, what they are or what they do.

It would seem that the hard-working, but uneducated, people behind the show think that a black hole is a gap among the stars, or perhaps a space whirlpool, through which one can scoot and return.

Actually, a black hole is a quantity of mass so great and so compressed as to produce a gravitational field that will let nothing escape, not even light. Anything moving too close to a black hole will fall in and be forever unable to emerge.

There are, indeed, some theories (not universally accepted) that, if a black hole rotates, matter falling in may emerge in a far different part of the Universe. Even then, however, any organized bit of matter such as a ship or a human being, or even an atom, is destroyed and will emerge as energy only.

A black hole can give rise to a number of highly dramatic situations— but you must understand it first.

And although children's shows need not necessarily be educational, it is surely not too much to ask that they not be miseducational.

To the general public, science fiction may seem to include the "super-man" story and, in fact, this can almost be justified.

"The Bionic Woman," for instance, traces the superpowers of its protagonist to the use of powered prostheses and of bionic organs with greater ranges of abilities than the living organs they replace.

One can imagine, without too much embarrassment, an artificial eye sensitive to a broader range of light-waves and to dimmer illumination than a natural eye is; to nuclear-powered limbs of supernormal strength and capable of great bursts of speed or thrust. Given that, one needs only imaginative plots and good acting (a big "only," of course) to have decent science fiction.

"Wonder Woman," on the other hand, is hopeless, since the conversion of an ordinary woman to a superkangaroo in red, white, and blue is achieved merely by spinning in place. (Superman at least stepped into a phone booth.)

"Wonder Woman" is mere fantasy, therefore, and can in no way be considered science fiction. . . . "Wonder Woman" might be saved if it took the attitude that the old "Batman" show did. In "Batman" the science was laughable, but it was used for that very purpose. "Batman" was deliberate farce, which made effective fun of many of the trappings of popular literature and of science fiction, too. And it becomes good science fiction to make fun of science fiction *knowledgeably*.

A very faint echo of that laughter is still to be found in the cartoon version of "Batman" which is on, for children, Saturday morning. A little mouselike creature "Bat Mite" is added, and, true to the tradition (from

Samson and Hercules onward) that supermuscles mean microbrains, Bat Mite is the only character in the cartoon that shows any spark of intelligence—and that must be on purpose.

Afterword

I was apparently wrong in my remark on *Star Wars*. I had only seen the motion picture once (not a dozen times, like some enthusiasts) and I had failed to notice, in the bar scene, that some of the characters *did* require alien conditions.

Well, I could wish that the producers and directors had emphasized that a bit more; but then I suppose they could legitimately express the wish that people like myself be a little more observant. No matter what my rationalization, I'm afraid I lose on that one.

◆

Insights and Outlooks

1. According to Asimov, what characteristics make good science fiction? Do you agree with him? Why or why not?

2. What criticism does Asimov have of audiences? How do you feel about this criticism? Do you think it is true? Explain.

3. How does Asimov reveal a sense of humour and slightly amused attitude toward his topic in this essay? What is your response to his attitude?

4. Choose a current movie, television program, book or story that claims to be science fiction and evaluate it according to Asimov's criteria. Present your findings in a written review of the selection.

A FLYING
START

◆

Margaret Atwood

Margaret Atwood is one of Canada's most distinguished authors and she has made innumerable public appearances over her career, but one of her most embarrassing moments came when she was only fourteen.

In adult life, my most embarrassing moments have come during other people's introductions to my readings. What do you do when the man introducing you proposes to read the audience the entire last chapter of your novel, gets your name wrong or characterizes you as some kind of machine-gun-wielding radical terrorist?

But my first moment of truly public embarrassment occurred when I was fourteen. It was the early days of CBC television, and things were kind of improvised. Many shows were live. There was usually just one camera; there was little editing. Much joy was contributed to the world, in those days, by the howlers, faux pas, bloopers and pratfalls that were sent out, uncensored, over the airwaves.

The woman who lived next door, and for whom I babysat, had some-how become the producer of a show called "Pet Corner," a title that is self-explanatory. At that time, in lieu of cats, I had a beautiful, green, intelligent praying mantis called Lenore (after the Poe poem, not after my future sister-in-law), which lived in a large jar, ate insects and drank sugar water out of a spoon. (For those who may accuse me of cruelty to insects, let me point out that this was, a) an old praying mantis, which had b) already laid its egg-mass, and which c) lived a good deal longer in my jar than it would have outside, as it was d) cold out there.) My neighbour thought this would be a good thing to have on "Pet Corner," so I went, praying mantis, spoon and all, and presumably electrified the audience with an account of what female praying mantises would eat if they could get any, namely male praying mantises.

Lenore was such a hit that "Pet Corner" decided to have me back. This time I was to be merely an adjunct. A woman was coming onto the show with a tame flying squirrel; I was to be the person the flying squirrel flew to, a sort of human tree.

All went as scheduled up to the time of the flight. Flying squirrels were explained, this one was produced (close shot), then raised on high, aimed and fired. But flying squirrels are nocturnal, and it was annoyed by the bright television lights. When it landed on me, it immediately went down my front.

At my school we wore uniforms: black stockings, bloomers, white blouses and a short tunic with a belt and a large square neckline. It was this neckline that the squirrel utilized; it then began scrabbling around beneath, and could be seen as a travelling bulge moving around my waistline, above the belt. (Close shot.) But it was looking for something even more secluded. I thought of the bloomers, and swiftly reached down the front of my own neckline. Then I thought better of it, and began to lift the skirt. Then I thought better of that as well. Paralysis. Nervous giggling. At last the owner of the flying squirrel fished the thing out via the back of my jumper.

Luckily the show went on during school hours, so none of my classmates saw it. Not much that has gone on at public readings since then has been able to compete in embarrassment value; not even the times I fell off the podium, had a nosebleed or had to be whacked on the back by James Reaney ("Harder!" I gasped. "Harder!") because I was choking to death. Maybe it's for this reason that I always have trouble spelling "embarrassment." I keep thinking it should have three e's.

———◆———
Insights and Outlooks

1. If you were in Margaret Atwood's shoes on "Pet Corner," what would you have done? How would you have reacted?

2. Did this story grab you? Did it hold your attention? What is it about the story, what techniques of writing, do you think make it a success? If you didn't like the story, why do you think it doesn't work?

3. Write your own "My Most Embarrassing Moment" memoir.

THE NATURE OF DAVID SUZUKI

◆

Jerry Buckley

David Suzuki "is passionate, driven, irreverent, brilliant, charismatic and controversial, usually all in the same sentence."

The bad news rolls off David Suzuki's tongue all too easily these days. Whether he is addressing business executives at a tiny downtown Toronto club or preaching to an anti-nuclear rally from the pulpit of a neighborhood church, Suzuki can't escape the grim statistics and dire predictions, evidence of what he considers man's mindless destruction of nature.

He talks of 3,000 acres [1214 ha] of rain forests being destroyed every day and the possibility that the world's wilderness areas will all be gone in 30 years. He cries out against the dioxins leaking into the Great Lakes, and he echoes the prediction that in just three years, one species of plant and animal will be going extinct every hour. "There have been times," he admits, "when I've felt, 'okay, that's enough. I'm going to buy a piece of land in British Columbia and go off and just live there.' And I still may." But Suzuki knows he can't do that, not now, perhaps never. "My anger is what sustains me," he says. "I'm too bloody mad."

Suzuki's anger, as anyone who knows him can attest, is genuine. Indeed, anger has been driving Suzuki for most of his years. A third-generation Japanese-Canadian, Suzuki spent three of his boyhood years, along with his sister, parents and grandparents, in a detention camp in British Columbia during World War II. That bitter memory has dominated his life and it helps explain why today he is a world-renowned geneticist, science popularizer, television star and environmentalist. "My father always told me that if I was going to compete with whites, I had to be ten times better," Suzuki says matter-of-factly. "He instilled in me a very powerful drive, that I had to achieve in order to be accepted."

In Canada, David Suzuki has achieved beyond even his most ambitious dreams. Everywhere from city playgrounds to prairie schoolhouses to Parliament Hill his name is now synonymous with science education and environmental activism. As host of "The Nature of Things With David Suzuki," a Canadian Broadcasting Corporation series, Suzuki has helped to demystify science for millions of Canadians and millions more around the world. With an eight-part series called "A Planet for the Taking," some years ago, he chronicled man's attempt to dominate nature—and brought the environmental problems of the world into stark view. . . . And he is passionate, driven, irreverent, brilliant, charismatic and controversial, usually all in the same sentence.

"Nobody can touch him in this country, and around the world he is in the same class as Carl Sagan and Jacques Cousteau," says Stuart Smith, past chairman of the Science Council of Canada, once the national advisory agency on science and technology policy. Says Pamela Stokes, director of Environmental Studies at the University of Toronto, "He puts science over in a way that people can understand, and he does it without demeaning it or making it all Mickey Mouse. Fifteen or twenty years ago, the general public didn't know or care much about science. Suzuki has been a big part of changing that."

"The Nature of Things" . . . attracts 1.3 million viewers each week, more than many of the drama shows carried by the CBC. The hour-long program is seen in the United States on PBS and in 80 other countries.

"Nature" covers a wide range of topics, from the dwindling population of cormorants in eastern Canada, to the fight between lumbermen and environmentalists over logging in the Queen Charlotte Islands in British Columbia, to the plight of the caribou in Labrador and northern Quebec, where 10 000 of the animals drowned some years ago. Whatever the topic, be it science, nature or medicine (programs have covered AIDS, and infant mortality in the Third World), the dominant theme is to question science and technology's impact on man and nature.

"We have become drunk with the power of our technology, and we have bought the illusion that we have control," Suzuki says. "It is estimated that there are 30 million species of plants and animals in the world, yet scientists have discovered only 1.7 million of them. How dare we think we can manage nature when almost 95 percent of it is a mystery?"

The crux of the problem, in Suzuki's view, is that the human species does not understand its position in nature. "Our whole definition of progress today is based on the notion that it is our role to dominate nature," he says. "If we come to understand weather, earthquakes, floods and oceans, we call that progress. But of course that progress is a total illusion because what science and technology provide is a very crude, but very powerful, way of subduing nature in the short run. But you don't manage it or control it in the long run. We are only a part of the universe."

Some critics contend that the wizardlike Suzuki is overly pessimistic, a doomsday prophet who exaggerates problems. "I think he goes overboard sometimes," says Louis Simonovitch, head of the Research Institute at Toronto's Mount Sinai Hospital and an old friend of Suzuki. "All of us are against technology that goes too far, but I'm not sure David has come to grips with where you draw the line. He wants to cut off a technology because it might be bad, but what about the good that it can do? It's fine to tell us that our values are screwed up and technology has gone wild. But we have to make choices."

The counter argument is that someone has to sound the warnings. Because Suzuki feels so strongly about the problems afflicting the natural world, says Michael Perley, director of the Canadian Coalition on Acid Rain, "he would rather go out on a limb that's a little shaky than not go out on a limb at all."

Indeed, there is a kind of fire in Suzuki's eyes when he talks about nature. A listener senses that no matter how many times Suzuki says it, his intensity remains at the same fever pitch. For Suzuki, butterflies and bald eagles, caribou and black bears, salmon and starfish and all creatures big and small are not simply words in a script, but each treasured parts of the universe.

And he still has the capacity to marvel at the natural world surrounding him. A few years ago, he was filming a show in the marshlands of Manitoba when, he recalls, he looked up to see dozens of flocks of geese moving south, making a wonderful noise as they went. "I knew that the marsh was part of the birds' migratory route, but I didn't know how beautiful the whole scene could be. I stood there looking at the sky and thought, 'My God, this is fantastic.' I was shivering with the thrill of it."

How this man came to be standing in a Manitoba marsh is best explained by looking back into his childhood.

"My father and Pearl Harbor."

That's Suzuki's answer when he is asked about the biggest influences in his life. "The most definitive event was Pearl Harbor," he says. "I was a Canadian, my parents were Canadian, but because of Pearl Harbor, Canada said we were the enemy." Unwelcome in British Columbia, where David had been born, the Suzukis moved east to Ontario.

But that didn't end the battle for young David. "I totally hated the Japanese people, but I couldn't avoid being one because the white society said, 'You're a Jap,'" he remembers. "So I grew up with a tremendous amount of self-hate. When I was a teenager, I wanted to have an eye operation, dye my hair and change my name to Smith. I was terrified of whites, terrified of rejection. The only thing I could do well was school work."

Academics was David Suzuki's tool for coping with his troubled world. And his most important mentor was his father, Carr, a laborer on a fruit farm. "I loved school," David recalls. "The worst thing my father could ever do to me was to threaten to take me out of school and put me to work."

There was never much question about the young David's future profession. "Right from the beginning, it was nature," Suzuki remembers. "My father was an avid collector of plants of all kinds. He used to go up in the mountains and bring back plants for his garden. Plus no matter where we lived, he always had a pond with fish and water life. It was his love of nature that made me want to be a scientist."

The shy, angry young man became the president of his high school senior class and an accomplished public speaker.

Then in 1954, Suzuki won a scholarship to Amherst College in Massachusetts. "Amherst was the best thing that ever happened to me," Suzuki says. "It was the kind of educational experience that was simply not obtainable [then] in Canada. It opened all my horizons."

Entranced by genetics, Suzuki went on to the University of Chicago for his doctorate and spent a year with the U.S. Atomic Energy Commission at Oak Ridge, Tennessee, before returning to Canada in 1962. As a professor of zoology at the University of British Columbia, he made his most significant scientific mark. Using the ordinary fruit fly, he demonstrated that in higher organisms, mutations exist in which genes can be controlled by simple factors like increases or decreases in temperature. Such mutations can be used to probe the mysteries of genetics, development and behavior.

But the more he learned as a scientist, Suzuki says, the more he realized he wanted to go beyond the lab and the classroom. "Scientists tend to be so focused on what they're doing, they're really not aware of the broader implications," he says. "I decided that it was not enough for scientists just to do good science, that you had to demystify your activity and warn the public of its implications."

Suzuki's media career began in earnest in 1969 when he hosted "Suzuki on Science," a half-hour science-oriented talk show. Two years later, he was asked to become the host of a science program to complement the already existing "Nature of Things." The program, "Science Magazine," attracted a big audience, running for five years before the two shows merged to become "The Nature of Things With David Suzuki."

Suzuki's television career has made him a star, but it has also humbled him. "My great conceit was that through the media, I was going to raise the public consciousness so they would take science more seriously and eventually vote for politicians who were more scientifically literate," Suzuki confesses. "But in terms of real political change and attitude toward science, there has been absolutely no effect. Our politicians are still every bit as ignorant about science as they were when I started."

One result is that Suzuki has in recent years shifted much of his emphasis to children. "Unfortunately, I don't believe adults are capable of changing very much," he says. "I've concluded that spending time hammering away at business people, for example, trying to get them to change, is far less productive than directing my energies at children who aren't already conditioned." Suzuki has written several books—includings ones on plants, insects, the senses, the body and weather—in a series aimed at giving children a hands-on look at science.

"The whole idea is to say to children that plants and insects are fascinating; they're not scary. They're important, and you can establish a relationship with them," Suzuki says. "The book on senses is to show them they are animals, too." Suzuki believes that when kids look at the world in this way, they will develop a different attitude toward nature. "I want children, when they see a chemical plant spewing junk into the air or water, to want to vomit. I want them to consider the water and the air and the soil their home," he says. "That may be airy, fairy, romantic talk, but I really believe the only way we're going to change the direction we're headed is to have that kind of spiritual connection with nature."

Suzuki is not one for grandiose statements, but he does admit to a certain sense of mission. "Yes, I have a mission, which is to point out what is so obvious—that the planet is in deep trouble and it's in deep trouble for one reason—us. At the rate we're going, we're headed straight down the tubes."

What to do? Maybe do nothing, says Suzuki. "My own sense is that the only long-term solution is not to touch the environment. I don't think you can get a technological solution to a technological problem. It's an endless treadmill. Every technology has a cost. You have to have faith in the enormous resilience and flexibility of nature. And," he adds, "we have to put our hope in the children."

◆

Insights and Outlooks

1. After reading this profile and perhaps drawing on your own knowledge, what is your impression of David Suzuki? If you had to provide a character sketch of him, what qualities and accomplishments would you stress?

2. Suzuki says, "We have become drunk with the power of our technology, and we have bought the illusion that we have control. . . . Our whole definition of progress today is based on the notion that it is our role to dominate nature." Do you agree with these statements? Point to specific examples to support your view.

3. David Suzuki suggests that the long-term solution may be to leave nature alone and allow it to heal itself. What do you think?

4. Design an observation research project where members of the class study one example of the impact of technology on nature within their community. Design an observation worksheet to guide the investigation and have each group report back to the class.

THE HUNTER
FROM 2000 BC

◆

Claudia Glenn Dowling, Traudl Lessing,
Tala Skari, Sasha Nyary

**What could we possibly learn from an anonymous man
who died over 4000 years ago?**

The man was a mountain climber and restless. In the valley homesteads the harvest of wheat and barley had been gathered in; the cattle and sheep and pigs wore the fat of summer. The ice of the glacier had retreated under the sun, and it was a good time for a man to hunt game in the forests or search for ore-rich rocks above the tree line, a good time to venture forth to trade or marry or fight with people who were hostile to him. He was no stranger to the mountains, this man, and he took what he would need in the high passes—a backpack, warm clothing, the makings of fire, his weapons. For the mountain, like the wild world below, was a dangerous place for a man alone. The weather, even in this golden season, could be perilous, with fogs and winds and sudden blizzards. But climbers expected that, and death can come to any man, early or late. It was perhaps only as he crouched on the ice 10,500 feet [3200 m] above the level of the sea, one arm outflung as if in supplication, that this man realized death had come for him.

And so he lay, pecked at by birds of prey and covered with the snows of passing centuries—until, in the fine, clear final weeks of another autumn, the warmest in memory, the ice that encased him melted away.

On September 19, 1991, Helmut Simon, a building superintendent from Nuremburg, Germany, and his wife, Erika, were climbing in the Alps along the border of Italy and Austria, as they had often done before. They assaulted Finail, making the summit at about midday, and then headed down toward Italy. They were walking along the Similaun glacier near the Hauslab Pass, backpacks in place, spiky metal crampons on their boots, when they had to leave the trail to avoid a puddle of melted snow. Erika, slightly behind her husband, suddenly stopped and cried, "There is something here in the snow." She looked more closely. "It's a man!"

Helmut was not repulsed by the man whose face was pillowed in the ice, or afraid. It is not unusual for climbers to find a body disgorged by a glacier. Helmut told himself, "He can no longer hurt you." And so he took some pictures. The man's relatives, Helmut thought, would want to know, once and for all, what had happened to him.

Helmut and Erika Simon had no idea that the unknown climber's kin had been dead for 4,000 years, or that the discovery of his almost perfectly preserved body would prove extremely important to his extended family—the family of humankind.

The couple made their way to a nearby refuge hut and told the warden there what they had seen. The warden telephoned the gendarmes in the Austrian village of Vent. They, too, were unsurprised. Just a month before, a married couple from Vienna who had died on a glacier in 1934 had been found and identified.

Two days later the man considered the best mountain climber in the world today, Reinhold Messner, happened by the hut on the Similaun glacier and heard of the discovery. "Nobody was really interested," he recalls. "Everybody said, 'It's a dead mountaineer, maybe fifteen or twenty years old.' Nobody took it seriously." But upon hearing that there were strange tools around the corpse, Messner and fellow climber Hans Kammerlander decided to take a look.

They found the man, his upper body sticking out of the glacier, his legs sunk in icy water. Messner could see the pores in the skin of the corpse and strange parallel markings on his back. He saw a bow, a shoe. He touched nothing (unlike some others who would follow him). "I've seen many, many dead bodies on high mountain peaks, but nothing like this," says Messner. "I realized immediately that this was an archaeological find."

It was two days before the rest of the world began to catch on. A forensic expert at Innsbruck University, Rainer Henn, was notified, but like the gendarmes he figured there was no rush to establish identity and cause of death. In any case, the weather socked in, and the Ministry of the Interior's helicopter couldn't fly in the fog. Finally, Henn got to the site, where he quickly understood that "this was no ordinary glacier corpse. Your typical glacier dead has fatty matter changed into wax and looks like a doll. This was something much older, a mummy." Henn and his crew hacked out a casket of ice to enclose the body, put it in a gunnysack and choppered it to an undertaker in the valley. The undertaker drove it to the university morgue in Innsbruck, where Henn's colleague Konrad Spindler, dean of the Innsbruck Institute for Prehistory, first saw the body.

"I was deeply moved," Spindler says of those first moments, which he calls the most exciting of his life. He examined the fine stitches of the leather clothing and shoes, lined with fur and an extra layer of hay for protection from the cold. He marveled at the knife with the one-and-a-half-inch stone blade. And he gazed with awe at the ax made of copper mixed with some other metal to harden the edge. His conclusion: This was a man from the Bronze Age, in the flesh.

In 1819 a Danish museum curator named Christian Jörgensen Thomsen designated the three ages of prehistory after the materials used during those eras to make tools: stone, bronze and iron. Stone Age people made axes and knives of flint. Later they found such metals as gold and copper. Extracted and then smelted from rock, gold was used only for decoration, while copper was sometimes shaped into tools. Then came the great discovery that copper mixed with about 10 percent of another metal, usually tin, would hold a better edge. The substance was what we now call bronze, and it made possible more efficient axes and sickles.

The rise of the Bronze Age was followed by the Iron Age, which saw the revolution of agriculture, commerce and war. Communities supported specialists, like miners to unearth the ore and smiths to smelt it. They made superior weapons, too, for armies to use to conquer and gain the resources they needed, and they formed governments to deploy those armies and built cities to dwell in. They passed down stories of their triumphs and rewarded the victors with luxuries—art and more precious metals. This was civilization.

The unknown climber, now officially designated the Prehistoric Man from the Hauslab Pass, lived at the beginning of this snowballing process of civilization in Central Europe. The great Middle Eastern civilizations had entered their Bronze Age a millennium earlier and had already flowered into city-states in what are now Iraq and the Indus Valley in Pakistan and western India. The pyramids of the Old Kingdom were standing in Egypt; in Britain the 1,000-year project of Stonehenge was under way. But in the Tyrol, people lived much as they had for centuries.

They dwelt in hamlets in the valleys. Their houses, typically one room with a hearth, were rectangles of posts sunk into the ground and thatched with branches. They hunted deer, birds, beavers, badgers and wild pigs. They traded their metals across the mountains. (The most significant impact of the Bronze Age was the expansion of trade routes, including those between Central Europe and other civilizations.) They raised grains and probably baked unleavened bread.

Since the people of the Tyrol had no writing and thus kept no records, details about everyday life have been gleaned from excavations of settlements and burial grounds. "We have a very large set of graves from the period," says Stuart Needham, the British Museum's curator of Bronze Age antiques. "But grave goods are conditioned by the rituals of burial—special garments and offerings. If this chappie was a victim of accident and not sacrifice, this tells us the other side of the story, the everyday."

This was no mere skeleton, found with ax heads and other ritual funeral artifacts. Here was a man of skin and blood and organs who had died carrying the stuff of daily life—not just stone and bronze but organic materials. For the first time, archaeologists could see real clothing of the era in fur and leather, see how feathers were fletched to the wooden shaft of an arrow, see that Bronze Age man used wood-framed backpacks like the *kraxen* used in the Tyrol today—until now believed to have been developed in the Iron Age, 12 centuries later.

"We had bones, of course, and pots and weapons. But here we've got a weapon where the wooden handle has survived, plus the binding which fixes the metal ax to the handle. This is the first example where you've really got it," says Christopher Stringer, the head of the human origins group at London's Natural History Museum. Stringer has consulted on exhibits of Lindow Man, recently unearthed from a peat bog in Cheshire, England. Until now, the oldest and best-preserved European corpses belonged to the bog people, dating roughly from 1000 B.C. to 200 A.D. But their tissues had been damaged by the very acids that preserved them.

The body of the unknown hunter is a very different proposition. It remained undisturbed because of a serendipitous series of climatic occurrences. When he died, the foehn—a warm, dry wind that blows for days—must have dehydrated and mummified the body. Then the snows came, and in time the world grew colder and the glacier covered him. Specialists think it unlikely that he moved downhill with the flow; they suspect that his body was trapped in a depression as the ice covered it. When global warming finally revealed his remains, all the new technologies of meteorology, archaeology, history, anthropology, chemistry, biology, medicine, anatomy and such esoteric combinations as paleo-ethno botany (the study of plant use in prehistoric times) could be brought to bear for the first time on a whole, organic man of the Bronze Age. Scientists could hardly contain themselves.

But first the body, thawing for five days since its discovery, had to be preserved. Mildew was already forming on the skin. They put the corpse back on ice again in the university morgue in Innsbruck, at a temperature of 21°F [–6°C], the same as the glacier's, and treated the hunter's body with a special disinfectant to arrest the growth of the fungus. There were fears, too, that the fungus, perhaps as old as the body, might fail to respond to today's chemicals. It was more than ironic that a body that had remained perfectly preserved for four millennia was deteriorating within a handful of days.

Critics called it shameful. And a flap soon erupted over how long it had taken the "experts" to realize what they had, and how amateurs had tampered with the body, removing it and its gear from the ice before they could be examined in situ. There were even reports in the Italian press about how the corpse had been turned over and made to wave at television cameras.

The arguments over who was to blame for mishandling the corpse—the warden on the mountain? curious climbers? Henn? Spindler?—rage on even as an international team of scientists descended on Innsbruck University to examine it. Among other enigmas are his tattoos—crosses on each knee, plus a series of parallel lines on his back. In other primitive cultures such inscriptions can delineate rank or clan membership or participation in rites of war, the hunt, puberty or courtship. "There may also be some magic involved in the man's tattoos," says Spindler. "But it is doubtful that we can usefully draw comparisons with other historic and primitive examples."

Once the preservers, photographers, radiologists and anthropologists have had their go, some incisions can be made. The most important will involve extracting a tiny sliver of bone for carbon 14 testing, a process used to date the Shroud of Turin. Although the experts seem to have few doubts that the find is genuine, only after that test, which should take several weeks, will the real age of the body be verified. Then the stomach, brain, intestines and blood cells can be sampled and a medical chart constructed. Superficially, the man appears not to have been wounded in a fall. The stomach's lining may show whether he froze to death and its contents whether he starved or, if he did not (as scientists hope), what he ate on the trail. His intestines may house parasites suggesting diseases of the era. His full set of teeth will provide more data about diet—if they have been ground in certain ways, for example, we will know he was primarily a grain eater. But the scientists' fondest hope is that the corpse is in good enough condition for a DNA analysis, which may reveal his genetic relationship to a specific group of modern-day Europeans.

His apparel and gear will be treated in Mainz, Germany, at the Roman-Germanic Central Museum, one of the most highly regarded institutes for this kind of restoration and preservation. X rays have already revealed at least 14 arrow tips inside the leather quiver. The question is: Are they made of bronze, stone or bone? The scientists in Mainz will also test the ax to determine what metal has been combined with the copper. Archaeologists hope that the ax's origins can be pinpointed by comparing it with other finds.

Meanwhile, there is a squabble over who inherits the discovery. At first it was believed that the hunter was on the Austrian side of the Tyrol, but he was so close to the border that it was difficult to be sure. Two Tyrolean villages nearest to the site claimed the body for display after preservation. But the Italian government of South Tyrol insisted that the man should reside in Bozen, that province's capital. And the hikers who originally stumbled across the body have retained a lawyer; he argues that it is a literal "treasure" and thus, by Italian, Austrian and German law alike, 50 percent of the value of the find belongs to the finder, 50 percent to the landowner.

A group of surveyors—three Austrians and one Italian—finally went to the site to ascertain, at least, who could claim land ownership. After sighting boundary markers, all agreed that the man was found on the Italian side. The Italians, presumably concerned about being blamed for the deterioration of the body, were quick to concede that, for the years it may take to study the prehistoric man, Innsbruck may house him. Said climber Messner, "Four thousand years ago there were no borders. He belongs to all of humanity."

And so, who is he, the man at the heart of the controversy? The explanations are just beginning to unfold. He was middle-aged for his era, 25 to 35 years old, with a clipped beard, fair hair and blue eyes. He was about five feet [1.5 m] tall with a brain as large as ours. He was probably well-to-do, as evidenced by his finely stitched leather clothes and his carefully crafted ax. He was bold and well prepared for the adventure that ended in his untimely death. And he will not rest in peace until the remaining questions about his death—and, more important, his life—have been answered.

◆

Insights and Outlooks

1. Based on the information in the article, why do you think this discovery of the Prehistoric man is particularly important? What can we learn from him?

2. What is your opinion of the squabble that erupted over who owns or inherits the discovery? Who do you think should benefit from the discovery? Who should be in charge of looking after the body? Explain your point of view.

3. Do you think the Prehistoric man should be put on public display? Why or why not?

4. If you could interview the Prehistoric man, what five questions would you ask him? Write down your questions and compare them with those of your classmates.

THE MUSE STRIKES
A MOTLEY CREW
———◆———

Peter McFarlane

**To write well, you must write
from the heart . . .**

Everyone is a writer. If I had any doubts about that fact before, they were dispelled when I began to work part time for a correspondence school specializing in journalism and short fiction.

The ad in the paper said the small Canadian company was looking for "published authors" to tutor students. I was a bit skeptical at first, but I was also broke and I had written one book, so I called the number and a woman explained that she paid tutors on a piece-work basis for what amounted to a day or two of work a week and offered to send me a sample batch of work.

A couple of days later, a courier delivered a bulky packet that included the school's handbook and the first assignments and "personal profiles" of a dozen students. When I glanced through them my original doubts seemed to be confirmed: the students were a bunch of hopeless dreamers.

The first was a heavy-equipment operator who wanted to write some of the amusing stories he'd collected during his 20 years on construction sites. The second was a homemaker who described herself as a born-again Christian and wanted to write inspirational pieces for *Reader's Digest*. The third was a single mother who explained that she wanted to write helpful hints and romantic stories. I tossed the work aside with the intention of sending it back to the school with a note explaining that I was not interested. But the note was never written. A few days later I picked up the work again and began to sift through the personal profiles where the students were asked, among other things, to describe their "most emotional experience."

I expected to be amused by bloated prose and sappy sentimentalism, but I was wrong. The students wrote of the birth of their children or the death of parents or, in one case, of holding an old dog as it slipped into its final sleep, with a disarming simplicity and thoughtfulness.

It was in a different light, then, that I read the reasons each had decided to take the course. Almost all said they had long harboured the idea of trying to write and many recalled being told that they were "natural writers" by teachers, parents or friends when they were younger.

But more important, they identified the root of their desire to write in their love of reading. They described their habits as if they were happily addicted, reading anything and everything for the sheer joy of that special soul-to-soul relationship that can be achieved only between a reader and a writer.

For two years now I have been the first reader for more than 200 aspiring Canadian writers. Aspiring, although I must admit not always inspiring. One young Maritime girl, for example, said she enrolled in the course in the hope of getting a "writer's pass" that would allow her to get into rock concerts free.

Then there was an obviously troubled Vancouver man who began a gory mystery story by having one of his characters burst through my office door and point a revolver at me with a warning that I had better watch what sort of assignments I gave him. Or else.

There were also a few whom I refer to as the Cranky Ones, the students who write aggressive religious tracts or bigoted essays on their least-favorite minority. But thankfully, sooner or later, these all seem to give up on the course and return to the much easier practice of haranguing their long-suffering family and friends face to face.

Most students are sincere and respectful of the craft. They stick with it and suffer through the barrage of rejections that are part and parcel of the writer's life. And while they struggle to get it right, I enjoy the weekly batch of stories and articles that offer a remarkable snapshot of the country. In any given week I might read about a one-armed model-ship builder from Saskatchewan, a highly liquid Yukon fishing trip, stories of a Ukrainian Christmas in Nova Scotia, the history of the rights of native women in Canada, reminiscences of the Dirty Thirties by a retired scrap dealer, a well-crafted cowboy story by an Alberta oil-rig worker and insightful articles on the Far East by a Canadian missionary living in Taiwan.

While the range of subjects is surprising, the quality, as one would expect, varies greatly. A few students still haven't learned how to make their nouns and verb agree. Others are addicted to the biggest, strongest and fastest adjectives or fall into the trap of trying to impress the reader by using a superabundance of elongated words.

But at the other end, there are writers of genuine talent and polish whose work could grace the leading magazines in the country.

A few of the stories and articles that pass across my desk do, in fact, make it into mass-market magazines. But most of those that are published find their way into small weeklies or literary publications where the pay barely covers the newly published writer's victory dinner at the local steak house.

For them it is enough. What motivates them is not money but a passion for the craft and a love of the written word. In a world that is dominated by the unrelenting sounds and flickering images of our audio-visual age, it is encouraging to find that the printed word which carries on a dialogue in perfect silence, still has a legion of dedicated followers.

I cannot always say the same thing about my fellow professional writers. The first day of the recent Writers Union of Canada conference in Ottawa was dominated by a fight for non-fiction writers to be classified as "creative documentary" writers and by a squabble between the fiction and "creative documentary" writers over the allocation of writers-in-residence grants.

I left the meeting early, and back at my desk I picked up the writing-school packet and glanced at the work of a new student, a retired pathologist who said he had trouble speaking because of a stroke. His most emotional moment, he wrote, came during the war when a shell hit close to the operating room where he was assisting in an operation. He was knocked down by the blast and his friend's head was blown off, with the veins still pumping spurts of blood.

The pathologist had been studying music in his native Austria when he was drafted into the German army and he wanted to tap into the simple power of the written word to share with others his love of music and the remembered horrors of war. Only the written word, which invites both reflection and contemplation, could serve his needs and he wanted to devote his declining years to getting it down and getting it right.

And that, put simply, is what writing is all about.

◆

Insights and Outlooks

1. How do you feel about writing? Do you find it a chore or struggle? Do you think you are no good at it and will probably never be or do you really enjoy it? What does this article suggest is the key to good writing? Would you agree? Does your answer change your attitude to your own writing?

2. Do you think that only writers whose work is good enough to be published should write? Why or why not? What is Peter McFarlane's attitude?

3. Our world is becoming more audio-visually oriented. Does this mean that the printed word as we know it will become less important? What do you think?

4. Identify a source of locally-produced writing, a school or community anthology or poetry collection for example. As a class, study some of the writing and see how it differs from the work of the professional writers you are used to studying.

THE GREAT KILLER WHALE DEBATE

Bruce Obee

How much do you know about killer whales?
Do you think they should be put on public display in aquariums?

When killer whales came into Victoria's Gonzales Bay it was always cause for excitement. A squadron would glide in from Juan de Fuca Strait, their ominous dagger-shaped dorsal fins slicing the sea like periscopes. With pockets full of rocks, my friends and I would clamber up the headlands and squint into the mist, watching, listening for that unmistakable gush of air exploding from their lungs. Any that surfaced within firing range were met by a volley of stones from our slingshots.

These were dangerous beasts. They could smash a rowboat to smithereens and swallow children in a single gulp. *Orcinus orca*, the notorious "black-fish," had no business in our bay, imperilling our safety. We resented these oceanic predators for their reputation, though we had never heard of anyone being attacked by killer whales. At the same time, we respected them for the fear they instilled in our adolescent hearts.

Like other typical west coasters in the 1960s, we blindly believed that orcas were bloodthirsty wolves of the sea, unfair competitors of our precious Pacific fishing industry. Though no one had ever studied them, they had been denigrated for a century: "In whatever quarter of the world the orcas are found, they seem always intent upon seeking something to destroy or devour," whaling captain Charles Scammon wrote in 1874.

Even the Canadian Department of Fisheries espoused the myth when, in 1961, it mounted a machine gun on the east shore of Vancouver Island to deter whales from entering the Strait of Georgia. Although the government's gun was never fired, shooting at killer whales from fishing boats was an acceptable pastime. One-quarter of the orcas caught for aquariums in the 1960s and '70s had bullet wounds.

The public showed little concern in the mid-1960s when killer whales from waters off British Columbia and Washington state suddenly became the hottest item for display in public aquariums. Not until the mid-1970s did scientists learn that "schools" of orcas are tight-knit families, or pods, that stay together for generations—a social organization unique in the marine mammal world. With the whales' ill-founded ignominy and the public's ignorance, there was no hint of the intense free-the-whales campaign that would ensue in years to come: the legal challenges, the efforts to foil captures at sea, the vociferous opposition to the incarceration of wild orcas. Today, the polarization is profound: while aquariums justify their activities on educational and scientific grounds, the staunchest opponents call for the release of "imprisoned" killer whales.

This long-simmering confrontation came to a head in February 1991 when Hyak, a 25-year-old whale at the Vancouver Public Aquarium, died. Then, four days later, a young trainer at Sealand of the Pacific in Victoria was killed by three captive orcas. Although unrelated, these incidents suddenly gave new prominence to the issue of whether killer whales should be on display in public and private aquariums.

Animal rights activists argue that Hyak's confinement was the cause of the whale's supposedly premature death. They cite studies which confirm that bull orcas off the B.C. coast may live 50 or 60 years. Aquarium managers counter that 43 percent of wild killer whales on the West Coast die in their first year of life, and the average lifespan of males that survive their first year is 29 years. Another argument, that unsanitary conditions in whale pools cause fungus and bacterial infections, which often kill captive orcas, has no scientific backing. However, scientists do know the immunity of whales is relatively weak compared to other animals. They have relatively small lymphatic systems for animals of their size and could therefore be particularly vulnerable to infections.

One obvious physical difference between captive and wild orcas is the "flaccid-fin syndrome." The dorsal fins of many captive whales flop to one side instead of standing upright, as do the dorsal fins of most wild orcas. The flaccid-fin aberration is particularly noticeable in captive males, but has been seen in only two wild orcas throughout the Pacific Northwest. Scientists surmise that the circular swimming patterns of captive whales may contribute to the disorder. Another theory suggests that captive orcas may spend more time resting at the surface, and without the support of the water for longer periods of time, their fins eventually become limp.

While there is no proof that confinement of orcas is physiologically harmful, it undoubtedly causes psychological stress, according to an expert witness at the inquest into the death of Sealand trainer Keltie Byrne. On February 20, 1991, the 20-year-old champion swimmer accidentally slipped into the orca pool. As she tried to climb out she was pulled back by a killer whale. Before she drowned, three orcas tossed her about for 10 minutes and one carried her underwater in its mouth. Dr. Paul Spong, a behavioural psychologist who has studied the sensory perception of orcas, testified that the whales' "bizzare and abnormal" behaviour was undoubtedly due to their confinement in "a condition of extreme sensory deprivation."

"You're not seeing a normal orca when you're looking at a whale in a tank," says Spong. Orcas rely largely on echolocation, and a whale in a tank is cut off from its typical acoustic environment. "It's terribly, terribly monotonous." Trainers have been injured by whales in other aquariums, he says, adding there has never been a verified unprovoked attack on humans by orcas in the wild. . . .

In 1964, the Vancouver Aquarium became the first institution to pay for the capture of a Pacific Northwest killer whale. In those days, orcas were thought to be too dangerous to exhibit live. So the aquarium hired a sculptor to kill an orca and use the carcass as a model to create a whale sculpture for public display. Moby Doll, as the unfortunate whale came to be known, was harpooned off Saturna Island in the southern Gulf Islands. The whale survived the wound and a number of rifle shots, so it was dragged across the Strait of Georgia and housed in a pen at Vancouver's Burrard Drydocks. The public was interested in seeing Moby Doll, yet seemed indifferent to its plight; this was, after all, an era when governments condoned the shooting of killer whales.

But the world's first captive killer whale was not the vicious predator people expected. It was gentle, even friendly, and soon researchers from across the continent were coming to visit Moby Doll. Among them was a biology student named Michael Bigg, who eventually became the world's foremost authority on killer whales. The whale won international acclaim before it died, three months after its inglorious capture. . . .

Killer whales are a good investment. At the Vancouver Aquarium, with an array of fish and marine life, sea otters, beluga whales, seals and tropical gardens, orcas are by far the main draw. Hyak, captured in 1968, was seen by 15 million people during the 23 years he was in captivity. In 1990, nearly a million people toured the aquarium. Although most visitors paid admission fees of between $5 and $8, the aquarium is not profit motivated.

"Our interests are the same as a museum; they are scientific and educational," says Dr. Murray Newman, the Vancouver Aquarium's director since 1956. Operated by a non-profit society, the aquarium spends almost $1 million a year on education and research.

"The significance of the aquarium," says Newman, "is to make people think about ecology, to make children think about what exists in nature." Books and films provide some insight, but nothing compares to a killer whale in the flesh, to hear its vocalizations, to watch it swim beneath the surface or leap clear out of the water. Children are most responsive to live whales, and once their curiosity is aroused they are eager to learn more of the broader picture, of the ecological needs of whales and other marine life, says Nancy Baron, head of the aquarium's education programs. Some 50 000 school children a year visit the aquarium. Baron says each new generation must be educated to see that the animals displayed in captivity are worth saving in the wild.

But Peter Hamilton, executive director of Lifeforce International, says incarcerating whales "desensitizes children to respecting these animals. It teaches them that it's okay for us to imprison whales just for our amusement." A former commercial artist, Hamilton formed Lifeforce in 1980 to oppose the use of animals for experimentation, entertainment and as food. The organization promotes replacing what it calls the "marine mammal slave trade" with rescue centres where sick or injured wild animals would be rehabilitated and released. With the backing of 2000 members, Hamilton's organization is the prickliest thorn in the side of the Vancouver Aquarium.

In 1990, Lifeforce went to court to try to block the aquarium's capture of three beluga whales. News reports indicated there was widespread public support for Hamilton's cause, but a survey commissioned by the federal government suggested otherwise. In 1989, before the capture permit was issued, pollster Angus Reid surveyed 1500 Canadians on their opinions about aquariums and captive beluga whales. Seventy-one percent favoured the capture of live whales for viewing and education. The strongest support—80 percent—was from British Columbia. Nation-wide, 75 percent endorsed whale research in aquariums. Again, British Columbia offered the strongest support with 82 percent.

Public sentiment about catching wild killer whales for display, however, may be quite different from that revealed in the beluga survey. The pure white beluga, with its placid, "grinning" face and docile manner, has a hypnotic appeal. Killer whales, on the other hand, are the most thrilling of all marine mammals, bursting through the surface with plumes of mist erupting from their blowholes. They have a commanding, militaristic appearance as they race along at speeds up to 50 kilometres an hour. They are the epitome of wild, free-roaming animals.

There is no way an aquarium can provide for the physical and social needs of such an animal, says Hamilton. The survival rate of captive whales has not been good, he says. While some have lived 12, 15 even 20 years or more, others have died within five or six years. Some have lasted only months.

However, it is difficult to compare wild and captive mortality rates, because there are not enough captive whales to provide a comparative sample, says John Ford, marine mammals curator at the Vancouver Aquarium. Mortality was significantly higher in the 1970s when aquariums were still developing husbandry methods for their orcas, notes Ford. But with today's knowledge, aquariums are better able to monitor the health of captive whales, to detect infections or illnesses at an earlier stage, and to develop antibiotics tailored to the whales. Success in keeping orcas alive depends on the aquarium, says Ford, but a 1987 study by Dr. David Bain at the University of California suggests that in the aquariums that provide the best care, mortality rates in the last decade are close to the death rate of wild whales. . . .

Taking advantage of the research opportunities provided by captive whales, Ford is conducting hearing tests of the aquarium's killer whales in co-operation with the U.S. National Marine Fisheries Service. In Alaska, whales are stealing sablefish off fishermen's lines before the catch can be hauled aboard. Scientists suspect the sound of the winches used to bring in the long lines attracts the whales to the boats. Several orcas have disappeared from the area, and some have been found bearing bullet wounds. By determining the whales' hearing capabilities, researchers hope to devise a method of masking the sound of winches. Ford is also trying to determine how the noise from increasing marine traffic affects movements of killer whales, which rely on faint echoes from their sonar systems to navigate and communicate.

This research is an example of how whales in aquariums can assist their wild counterparts, says Ford. However, he has reservations about keeping captive whales purely for entertainment and profit. His view is shared by Graeme Ellis, a marine mammals technician at Nanaimo's Pacific Biological Station. Ellis, who has studied West Coast orcas since 1968, was a member of the Sealand team that captured several orcas in 1970, including a rare albino. He was also among the first to swim with wild killer whales and has worked as a trainer.

"There's a fine line between education and entertainment," says Ellis. When he was a trainer, Ellis became disillusioned by tourists who got angry when whales failed to perform as expected. There were huge profits to be made, and whales were forced to do the same tricks hour after hour, day after day. "I don't think those animals deserve to be sacrificed for entertainment," he says.

Ellis's knowledge of wild killer whales is intimate. He worked closely with Dr. Mike Bigg, who pioneered a system of identifying orcas through photographs of fins, saddle patches and scars. Bigg died of cancer in 1990, but his legacy is a wealth of knowledge about family relationships among Pacific Northwest killer whales. Through thousands of photographs, 64 orca pods with a total of about 380 whales have been identified and given alphanumeric names, says Ellis. Each pod is an extended family comprised of matrilineal groups. . . .

In the late 1970s, Ford discovered that each resident pod has its own "dialect" consisting of repeated phrases that are passed down through generations. With a network of hydrophones and radio transmitters, pods can be identified and tracked through recordings of their vocalizations. A hydrophone can pick up the voices of whales six or eight kilometres away. Paul Spong, who has several hydrophones in the Johnstone Strait area, says that after 23 years of segregation at San Diego Sea World, Corky still speaks the language of its Pacific Northwest family. . . .

Since 1980, Jim Borrowman and Bill Mackay of Stubbs Island Charters have been running summer whale-watching and nature cruises out of Telegraph Cove, a seven-hour drive from Victoria. Growing public interest in whales has expanded the business: in 1989 they invested $1 million in a second ship, and, at $65 for a five- to seven-hour trip, the cruises attract steady business.

Borrowman, whose livelihood depends largely on wild orcas, would not seem a likely defender of the capture of whales. But he says children become easily bored watching the dorsal fins of wild whales from a distance. They prefer aquariums, where they can see the whales at close range. He is convinced that if aquariums stop educating children, the growing appreciation for wild orcas will diminish: the unenlightened attitudes of the 1960s could reappear. "It would be nice if there were no captive whales, but I'm afraid of what might happen in the future without them," says Borrowman.

Alex Rhodes, owner of Sea Coast Expeditions in Victoria, agrees that watching wild whales appeals more to adults than children, but he disagrees that captive orcas inspire an appreciation of whales on the high seas. "We try to keep the experience in its proper context, to make sure people understand we're dealing with wild whales, not animals that are friendly toward humans."

On Rhodes's seven-metre, high-speed inflatable boat we encounter wild orcas along the southern shore of San Juan Island, 30 kilometres out of Victoria Harbour in American water. Suddenly the dorsal fin of a big bull slices the surface barely 10 metres from the boat, followed by a smaller whale. Biologist Pam Stacey recognizes the stubby fin and unusually loud breathing. This is Spieden, official J8, a grandmother estimated to be nearly 60 years old. Stacey confirms the identification from a photograph in a genealogical registry compiled by orca researchers. The bull is Spieden's brother, Ralph, known also as J6. Three other whales from his family appear—Spieden's 34-year-old daughter, Mamma, and her two offspring, Blossum and Shachi—swimming off our starboard bow.

There are others, and Stacey explains that we are surrounded by J pod, four matrilineal groups totalling 18 whales. Cameras click furiously as the killer whales bob upright with their enormous heads in the air, flap their flukes and pectoral fins on the surface, and even leap right out of the water.

"This is the best $70 I ever spent," says a beaming Mark Greaves, who travelled from England intent on seeing wild killer whales. A member of Greenpeace U.K., he considers the confinement of whales cruel, and steadfastly refuses to view them in aquariums. I admire his decisiveness. But I have witnessed the excitement of my two young daughters as they look through the glass at the Vancouver Aquarium into the tiny eyes of live orcas. And I have shared their apprehension and awe at the sight of wild killer whales approaching our boat as we cruise the waters off southern Vancouver Island. While my pragmatic side appreciates the value of captive whales, my emotions say it is wrong. These orcas are not fish, they are mammals with families, much like ours. We have the ability to separate them, but do we have the right? Today, with wild whales blowing a stone's throw from the boat, I feel my pragmatism yielding to my emotions.

Elated, we reluctantly head back to Victoria. As we pass Gonzales Bay, I recall the times my friends and I shot at those "dangerous" beasts with our slingshots, and it seems my desire to fire at them faded with my adolescence and ignorance. It was not until today, listening to Pam Stacey, that I realized that as a Vancouver Islander I have watched this same pod of whales many times from the shore over the last 40 years. My own children have seen the offspring of the same wild whales I watched as a youngster. Two families, growing up together on the same coast.

◆

Insights and Outlooks

1. Did this article tell you anything about killer whales that you didn't know before? Did it change your ideas about them or your attitude toward them?

2. In small groups, develop a chart of pro and con arguments on the topic of whether killer whales should be kept in captivity. You can draw on points from the article and from your own reading or experience. Discuss the arguments in your group and try to come to a group decision.

3. Do you think it is true that children need to see animals close-up in captivity to appreciate and learn about them? What role do you think aquariums and zoos should have? Can you suggest any alternatives?

4. Do some research on another animal often kept in aquariums or zoos. Explore its nature, habits, and its natural environment. What effect do you think captivity might have on it? Try to support your position with evidence and present your findings to the class for discussion.

FEEDING MONSTERS
WITH OUR YOUNG

——◆——

Stephen Strauss

"AIDS is not the Big Unfriendly Giant, or child abuse, or mass murder. AIDS is an illness. Its only evil is that too many die too young."

This is a story about children and AIDS, and grown-ups and truths unsaid and apparently unsayable.

My 11-year-old daughter was chosen to give the graduation speech for her Grade 6 class. Somehow it seems important to note that hers is a school full of Parminders and Trans and Rondres—a place built on a notion of diversity, which it celebrates in Black Pride Week and Chinese New Year and any number of commemorations of the worth of difference.

Annie was delighted with her honour and quickly began writing her oration. But as she often does, she came to me with the piece half-penned and asked what I thought, and wondered what more she could add. Now there is a great temptation for a father who is a writer to take over here, to transform himself from the best of all things—a caring parent—to the worst of all things—a know-it-all editor.

However, what she had written was so transparently and wondrously 11—a recounting of the time she made her monkey face and had the Grade 2 class laughing hysterically even though they were kept after school, the time the fourth-grade class read Roald Dahl's *BFG* (Big Friendly Giant) and everyone loved it, and her personal choice of favourite teachers—that I wanted simply to kiss her and pronounce: God bless this child. But because she believed that the speech needed to be a bit longer, I asked whether anything bad had happened.

The vice-principal died of AIDS three years ago, she said.

Maybe you should mention that, I told her.

So she wrote that there had been one tragedy in her years in school. The vice-principal died of acquired immune deficiency syndrome. Everyone was sad, and it showed that bad things could happen to good people.

Annie went off to school with the speech the next day and came back quite happy. Her teacher had loved it, but there was one problem. She wasn't allowed to say the vice-principal had died of AIDS. She wasn't sure exactly why.

But I was curious enough to march off to the school the next day and ask for an explanation. The current vice-principal provided a rationale in several parts.

First, he said that as all the parents did not know the cause of his predecessor's death, he didn't want to drop a "bombshell" on them at graduation. Interesting, I responded, but it appeared that it wasn't a secret to kids' information underground, and Annie's speech was talking to and for kids.

Well, he continued, the AIDS victim himself hadn't officially told people what his illness was and had maintained to the end that he was going to get better. Moreover, he had hidden the illness even from his family, including his mother.

My head started nodding like those dipping ducks street-corner vendors sell. What sadness. A hidden life with horrors too terrible to admit even in death. Nonetheless, I responded that this happened three years ago. Times had changed. And wasn't it clear the only reason we were censoring the cause of death was that it wasn't a heart attack or a car crash but AIDS?

Well, the vice-principal said, if the man had killed his family and then turned the gun on himself, would Annie have mentioned that in her speech? My jaw gaped. Was he suggesting that having AIDS was somehow like murdering your family and then killing yourself? Oh, no, no, no, no, he said. But all the no's sounded like yes's to me.

I said the beauty of having the reference made as Annie had done it was that it made AIDS so normal. Nothing was dwelt on. No position was taken, except that these things happen and they sadden us. Like the happy memory of the BFG or the giggles over the monkey face, it was life. And wasn't that exactly the psychic soil schools wanted prepared for their larger AIDS education efforts?

Well, yes, the vice-principal answered, but if we were talking about normalizing situations, did that mean that if there were children in the school who were sexually abused by their parents—and believe you me there were—that we should tell everyone their names?

What? Was he implying that having AIDS was somehow akin to sexually abusing your children? Again a chorus of false-sounding no's. We debated some more and nothing changed, and when I had to go to work, he said he would discuss the issue again with the teachers. I shrugged. One of the fruits of a life in journalism is the ability to see kiss-offs coming from 10,000 miles away.

After the encounter, I was torn. Wrong is always somewhat right. The vice-principal truly believed that he was protecting both a dead man's honour and living children's sensibilities. And who was I to insist that Annie "out" a person against his wishes?

And all my disdain for systematic hypocrisy kept colliding with the first commandment of parenthood: Don't louse up your children's life to make a point. So in the end I did nothing.

And that's how it might have ended if it weren't for Devorah Berman Kleinman. In one of those eerie synchronies that make us think there must be a larger meaning to life, I came after the hot happy graduation to be reading Mrs. Kleinman's hurt-filled letter in The New York Times about the death of her husband from AIDS. She spoke of being treated as a pariah, and of the failure of friends and relatives to transcend the letters A-I-D-S and simply feel for a human pain. The letter ended with the poetic sentence, "This disease has such monsters attached to it, why feed those monsters?"

I found myself half-crying for her, and for Annie's dead vice-principal and the craziness we have collectively built into our psyches. What is wrong with this society that we can accept a hundred different cultures, but produce a disease that cannot speak its name? Yes, it is true that in announcing the cause of his death we in a way would have sexually "outed" this particular individual. And it is true that AIDS troubles people in ways other diseases do not—but true education is always about change. The taboos must end some place. All those school AIDS-awareness programs with their emphasis on what covers what and what goes into what will ultimately fail if we can't purify our prejudiced hearts.

AIDS is not the Big Unfriendly Giant, or child abuse, or mass murder. AIDS is an illness. Its only evil is that too many die too young. Eleven-year-olds can know that. And their parents. And the parents of all the dead and dying.

Parminder and Rondre and Tran and Annie will understand, but only if they can speak what is.

--------♦--------
Insights and Outlooks

1. Do you think Annie should have been able to mention the cause of the vice-principal's death in her speech? Why or why not?

2.   How did Annie's attitude to the vice-principal's death differ from her father's and the current vice-principal's? What do the differences in attitude reveal?

3.   How young is too young to be educated about AIDS? Do you think you need to know about AIDS? Why or why not?

4.   Discuss the meaning of the following, "This disease has such monsters attached to it, why feed the monsters?"

A HARD LIFE
BUT A BETTER ONE

◆

Chui-Ling Tam

**What would it be like to come to a totally new country
and make a new life?**

My aunt married her sweetheart of 12 years last week. It was a simple wedding at home, with a justice of the peace who intoned the marriage vows in words they didn't understand.

That didn't matter. She knew when it was time to say "Yes," and she said it—emphatically—in a tight, hard voice that suppressed 12 long years of waiting to start her new life in Canada with her husband and family. Beside her, my new uncle grinned foolishly in relief a scant three days before his 90-day grace period with immigration expired. It was the first time I'd seen him smile since he arrived from China.

It may seem strange for two people to wait 12 years to marry, but it was the price my aunt paid to leave her homeland, where she met her husband on a state farm in their late teens. She would not have been allowed to leave if they had married in China.

My aunt was the last member of my mother's family to come to Canada, by grace of the reunification program introduced in 1988. She came in search of a better life, and in the modest home she shares with her two younger sisters, her brother-in-law and her father, she has found it. . . .

Many Southeast Asian immigrants arrived in the 1970s—and arrive still in the 1990s. My family was part of that herd . . . We had little worldly wealth to lose. When we landed in Ottawa in 1972, we had about $100 in cash, and all we left behind, besides a rather extensive family and numerous friends, was a little two-room shack that passed for our home.

My mother has worked at the same restaurant for the past 18 years, and my father has hopped along a string of jobs in other people's restaurants. They did not take a vacation until two years ago, and they did not go anywhere when they did. They couldn't afford it.

But they don't mind. My older brother and I are working—not in kitchens—and my younger brother and sister are in university. My parents now live in a red-brick bungalow surrounded by trees in a quiet suburb of Ottawa. They have running water, a 28-inch colour television and a car.

It's a far cry from the two-room home we left in Hong Kong, which had no running water. As a child of five, I recall trooping off to the big black outhouses down the street and the hordes of women and children who washed and bathed in the common watering area near our house.

When a thunderstorm knocked out the roof in the front room, the whole neighbourhood pitched in to attach a new corrugated-iron roof, and the air reeked with the smell of tar.

Not speaking English and with only a high-school education, my parents never expected to find comfortable jobs. Some days, my mother doubts whether her life would have been any harder in Hong Kong, where she worked for a time at a laundromat. She knew the life of riches was long behind her, ever since the Chinese Communists forced her family to give up their mansion and servants in Canton.

Often, before my grandparents and aunts arrived in 1985, my mother would talk wistfully of them, never expecting to find the money to make the trip back. The last time I gave her roses, she told me that the blooms were more fragrant in China.

But I don't think my parents ever regretted their choice. They have friends and family in Canada, and their children will never know the life they had.

Canada hasn't been wonderful. The winters are hard, the work is hard, and the range of services is bewildering to a Chinese-speaking couple. In leaving Hong Kong, my parents gave up some of their independence. They rely on their children to help them with finances and visits to the doctor, or choosing paint and wall paper at hardware stores.

My mother often stares at her knotted hands and murmurs that when she was a young woman, she had long, beautiful hands. Two decades of dishwashing and cooking eight hours a day, six days a week, have left brown spots from splashing grease.

Today, she and my father are both worried about how long their aging bodies can continue such work.

For all that, they have a good life. They have a comfortable home and enough to eat. They can brag about their children to friends. Their son, the pilot, their daughter, the journalist, their younger son and daughter, the university students. Very probably, my aunt and her husband will have a similar life. She works as a seamstress and he at a laundromat. They expect, and ask, for little more. It is enough that they can choose their lives, that their children will have an education and perhaps work in offices rather than endure the hard labour of state farms in China, or the hot kitchens and dirty hotel toilets in Canada.

I expect that they will brag about their children in 25 years, as do my parents. And they will quite likely have their own home and be grateful that after 12 long years, they were finally able to start the family they wanted for so long in a country where they could decide their future.

Their life will be hard, but I doubt that they will ever regret the loss of their homeland. While Canada is not the land of milk and honey, it offers them a lot more worldly wealth and freedom than China ever could.

----◆----
Insights and Outlooks

1. What thoughts and feelings do you have about the Chinese couple described in this article? Are you also a relatively recent immigrant or do you know recent immigrants? Discuss their experiences.

2. Why do you think people choose to come to Canada? What has Canada to offer? What hardships or difficulties might new immigrants face? Why?

3. If you were to give advice to a new immigrant arriving in Canada, what would you consider the most important information you could share? Why?

4. Interview a recent immigrant or describe your own experiences and report to the class on how the transition to life in Canada was difficult or easy.

TEXT CREDITS

———◆———

Page 2: Reprinted from *Canoe*, October 1989, with permission of Canoe America Associates, Kirkland, Washington.

Page 6: Reprinted from *Zoot Capri, the Magazine*, Fall 1991 issue, copyright —The Alberta Alcohol and Drug Abuse Commission.

Page 10: Taken from A CHILD IN PRISON CAMP © 1971 Shizuye Takashima, published by Tundra Books.

Page 14: Copyright Christine Welsh from the book *Women in the Shadows* to be published by Douglas & McIntyre. First appeared in *Canadian Literature* Winter 1991.

Page 22: From WE ARE STILL MARRIED. Copyright © Garrison Keillor, 1982, 1983, 1984, 1985, 1986, 1987, 1988, 1989, 1990. Reprinted by permission of Penguin Books Canada Limited.

Page 25: First printed in *Ms.* Magazine. Copyright © Mariah Burton Nelson.

Page 29: From LOVE & MARRIAGE by Bill Cosby. Copyright © 1989 by Bill Cosby. Used by permission of Doubleday, a division of Bantam Doubleday Dell Publishing Group, Inc.

Page 34: From *Newsweek*, June 27, 1990. Copyright © 1990 by Judy Blume. Reprinted by permission of Harold Ober Associates Incorporated.

Page 37: From *Between Ourselves: Letters Between Mothers and Daughters, 1950–1982*, edited by Karen Payne. Copyright © 1983. Reprinted by permission of Michael Joseph Ltd. and Pelham Books.

Page 40: Copyright © 1992 by Playing With Time Inc.

Page 48: *Seventeen* / James Thornton.

Page 53: From *Seeing Ourselves: Exploring Race, Ethnicity and Culture* edited by Carl E. James, 1989. Copyright © Adrienne Shadd. Reprinted by permission of the author.

Page 58: Copyright © Robert Fulghum, "A Bag of Possibles and Other Matters of the Mind," *Newsweek: Special Issue: How to Teach Our Kids* (September 1990): 92. Used with permission.

Page 66: Reprinted with permission—The Toronto Star Syndicate.

Page 72: Reprinted from OPEN NET by George Plimpton, by permission of W. W. Norton & Company, Inc. Copyright © 1985 by George Plimpton.

Page 82: Reprinted with permission from the November 1990 *Reader's Digest*. Copyright © 1990 by The Reader's Digest Assn., Inc.

Page 88: This article originally appeared in *Canadian Musician* magazine, June, 1990, Volume XII Number 3. Reprinted with permission of the Publisher.

Page 96: Copyright The Observer, Chelsea Bridge House, Queenstown Road, London, England.

Page 100: From *Equinox*, July/August 1991. Reprinted by permission of the author.

Page 104: "Oil and Water", from OUT HERE by Andrew Ward. Copyright © 1991 by Andrew Ward. Used by permission of Viking Penguin, a division of Penguin Books USA Inc.

Page 109: Reprinted from SHE MAGAZINE/National Magazine Co.

Page 114: Reprinted by permission of the author, Richard Skinulis.

Page 119: From *Inventors at Work: Interviews with 16 notable American inventors* by Kenneth A. Brown. Published by Tempus Books of Microsoft Press, a division of Microsoft Corporation. Copyright © 1992 Kenneth A. Brown.

Page 128: Reproduced, with permission, from THE FUTURIST, published by the World Future Society, 7910 Woodmount Avenue, Suite 450, Bethesda, Maryland 20814.

Page 133: Reprinted with permission from the January 1991 *Reader's Digest*.

Page 138: Reprinted with permission from *Maclean's*, February 24, 1992 issue.

Page 142: Judith Stone/© 1991 Discover Magazine.

Page 149: Reprinted with permission—The Toronto Star Syndicate.

Page 153: David Van Biema, Steven Petrow, Tala Skari/*Life* Magazine © 1992 The Time Inc. Magazine Company. Reprinted with permission.

Page 160: "What Makes Good Science Fiction?" copyright © 1977 by Triangle Publications, Inc. Reprinted from TV Guide from ASIMOV ON SCIENCE FICTION by Isaac Asimov. Used by permission of Doubleday, a division of Bantam Doubleday Dell Publishing Group, Inc.

Page 165: "A Flying Start" by Margaret Atwood from *That Reminds Me . . . : Canada's Authors Relive Their Most Embarrassing Moments* by Marta Kurc. Published by Stoddart Publishing Company Limited. Reprinted with permission.

Page 167: Copyright 1988 National Wildlife Federation from the September/ October 1988 issue of *International Wildlife.*

Page 173: Claudia Glenn Dowling, Traudl Lessing, Tala Skari, Sasha Nyary/ *Life* Magazine © 1991 The Time Inc. Magazine Company. Reprinted with permission.

Page 180: Reprinted by permission of the author.

Page 184: From *Canadian Geographic* January/February 1992. Reprinted by permission of the author. Bruce Obee is author of *Guardian of the Whales: The Quest to Study Whales in the Wild.*

Page 192: *The Globe and Mail.*

Page 196: Originally published in *The Globe and Mail,* July 25, 1991.

Every reasonable effort has been made to trace the original source of reprinted material in this book. Where the attempt has been unsuccessful, the publisher would be pleased to hear from copyright holders to rectify any omission.

PHOTO CREDITS

———◆———